Almost Beauty

Also by SUE SINCLAIR

Heaven's Thieves
Breaker
The Drunken Lovely Bird
Mortal Arguments
Secrets of Weather & Hope

Almost Beauty
NEW AND SELECTED POEMS

SUE SINCLAIR

icehouse poetry
an imprint of Goose Lane Editions

Copyright © 2022 by Sue Sinclair.
Introduction copyright © 2022 by Ross Leckie.

All rights reserved. No part of this work may be reproduced or used in any form or by any means, electronic or mechanical, including photocopying, recording, or any retrieval system, without the prior written permission of the publisher or a licence from the Canadian Copyright Licensing Agency (Access Copyright). To contact Access Copyright, visit accesscopyright.ca or call 1-800-893-5777.

The selected poems were originally published in the following editions: *Secrets of Weather & Hope* (London, ON: Brick Books, 2001), *Mortal Arguments* (London, ON: Brick Books, 2003), *The Drunken Lovely Bird* (Fredericton, NB: Goose Lane Editions, 2004), *Breaker* (London, ON: Brick Books, 2008), *Heaven's Thieves* (London, ON: Brick Books, 2016)

Edited by Ross Leckie.
Cover and page design by Julie Scriver.
Cover image: *Wise Woman*, copyright © 2020, by Amy Stewart, acrylic on canvas, 101.6 x 76.2 cm. www.amystewartartist.com.
Printed in Canada by Hume Media.
10 9 8 7 6 5 4 3 2 1

Library and Archives Canada Cataloguing in Publication

Title: Almost beauty : new and selected poems / Sue Sinclair ; edited and with an introduction by Ross Leckie.
Other titles: Poems. Selections (2022)
Names: Sinclair, Sue, 1972- author. | Leckie, Ross, 1953- editor.
Identifiers: Canadiana (print) 20210368470 | Canadiana (ebook) 20210368683 | ISBN 9781773102344 (softcover) | ISBN 9781773102726 (EPUB)
Classification: LCC PS8587.I55278 A6 2022 | DDC C811/.6—dc23

Goose Lane Editions acknowledges the generous support of the Government of Canada, the Canada Council for the Arts, and the Government of New Brunswick.

Goose Lane Editions
500 Beaverbrook Court, Suite 330
Fredericton, New Brunswick
CANADA E3B 5X4
gooselane.com

Contents

9   Introduction by Ross Leckie

NEW POEMS

23   *The Prado*
24   *Shall We Gather*
25   *Hey Nonny Nonny*
27   *The Peonies*
28   *Reprieve*
29   *Pastoral*
30   *The Nashwaak River*
32   *Tungsten Mine*
33   *Overburden*
35   *The Mine Speaks*
36   *Tokens*
38   *Ampersand*
39   *Exposé*
40   *It Could Happen to Anyone*
42   *Sex Ed Just Got Weirder*
43   *Thoughts and Prayers*
44   *Birth of Mars*
45   *Ultrasound*
46   *Service*
47   *Strange Heaven*
48   *The Washing Place*
49   *Long Haul*
51   *To the Farmers Hand-Pollinating Pear Trees in Hanyuan County, China*
52   *The Most Important Room in the World*

SECRETS OF WEATHER & HOPE (2001)

57   *The Pitcher*
58   *Green Pepper*
59   *Red Pepper*
60   *Upstream*
61   *Lilies*
63   *André Kertész*
64   *Lyric Strain*
65   *Red and Orange Streak by Georgia O'Keeffe*
66   *Toronto Skyline*
67   *Stratus*
68   *Cirrus*
69   *Cirrus Radiatus*
70   *Stratocumulus Undulatus*
71   *Domestic Habits*
72   *Springtime*
73   *The Scent of Wolf Willow*
75   *March*
76   *Grazing*
77   *Departure*

MORTAL ARGUMENTS (2003)

- 81 *Birthday*
- 82 *Prime*
- 83 *Vacation*
- 84 *Witness I*
- 85 *Springtime*
- 86 *Paddling*
- 87 *Witness II*
- 88 *Roses*
- 89 *Dreamlife of Houses*
- 90 *Witness III*
- 91 *Cityscape*
- 92 *Love Poem II*
- 93 *Wickaninnish*
- 94 *Poem*
- 95 *Love Poem IV*
- 96 *Days in Between II*
- 97 *Flatrock, January 1, 2002*
- 98 *Sympathy*
- 99 *Wolastoq, Spring*
- 100 *War in Other Countries*
- 101 *Shelter*
- 102 *Illusion*
- 103 *June 15*
- 104 *Extinction*
- 106 *English Daisies*
- 107 *Atget:* The Milkman's Horse
- 108 *Second View of Bell Island, October 2001*
- 109 *First Snow*
- 110 *Night Fare*
- 111 *Forever*
- 112 *Third View of Bell Island, December 2001*
- 113 *Nocturne*

THE DRUNKEN LOVELY BIRD (2004)

- 117 *Lilacs*
- 119 *Streetlight, Afternoon*
- 121 *City Hall, August*
- 122 *Jellyfish*
- 123 *Cottonwood*
- 124 *Refrigerator*
- 126 *Bathtub*
- 127 *Moratorium*
- 128 *Before You Were Born*
- 129 *In Season*
- 130 *No One Asks Leda to Dance*
- 132 *Goldfish*
- 133 *Solanaceae* Datura
- 138 *Photograph of My Mother as a Child or Invitation to the Wedding*
- 140 *Barbershop*
- 141 *The Drunken Lovely Bird*
- 143 *Orpheus Meets Eurydice in the Underworld*
- 144 *Home from Danceland*

BREAKER (2008)

149 *Surrender*
150 *Wonder*
151 *We Hope It Will Be Quick*
152 *Pawel Laughing on the Beach*
153 *Days without End*
154 *Vanity*
156 *Dead Pelican, Point Lobos*
157 *Fish*
158 *Big East Lake*
159 *Breaker*
160 *Away*
162 *Into the Open*
163 *Nesting*
164 *Fourth View of Bell Island, January 2, 2003*
165 *Endurance*
166 *View from the Train*
168 *At Grenadier Pond*
170 *Exposed*
172 *Quiet*
173 *Tell It to the Night*
175 *Evening*
176 *Suburbs*
177 *Waiting*
178 *Waiting for the Forks*
180 *Breakwater*
181 *Falling from a Great Height*
182 *Sixth View of Bell Island*
183 *Longing*
184 *Asleep*

HEAVEN'S THIEVES (2016)

187 *Winter in the Garden*
188 *Heaven's Thieves*
189 *Ends of the Earth*
190 *Loving Pavlova*
192 *Oranges for Adorno*
193 *The Invention of Beauty*
194 *1st Corps de Ballet*
195 *Red Dye No. 40*
197 *On the Meditations*
199 *Missing*
200 *Fear of Wasps*
201 *How to Be Hungry*
202 *Notre-Dame de Paris*
204 *Guardians*
205 *Exercise in Beauty No. 2*
207 *Cherry Trees*
208 *Summer, Madrid*
209 *Mezquita–Cathedral*
211 *Between Heaven and Earth*
212 *Prelude*
214 *Poem for Nietzsche's Eyes*
215 *What Can I Tell You*
216 *My Name*
218 *Visited*
219 *The Dead*

223 **Acknowledgements**

Introduction

ROSS LECKIE

I
Things Are Not as They Appear

Sue Sinclair's poetry reads with a pleasurable elegance, lush and simple, but in this reading pleasure we can lose sight of its complexities. We lose sight; we don't see with the attention the poems require of us. This is not because we are lazy, though we may well be, but because paying attention is far more difficult than our grade-three teachers expected it to be. The poems are a kind of origami in language. The paper crane sits on the table before us, and we see its poise, sense that it is as light as a feather and is about to lift off across the lake and over the wooded hills to another lake we cannot see. However, simultaneously, it announces that it is a made thing, evident in the folded paper of its making. It is plain as day, we think, this exchange between exterior and interior.

But to unfold a poem and see all the things enfolded in it is a form of transgression and a form of love. It dispels the magic of its being, encroaches on its privacy. It turns folds into creases. Yet it also lets it know you care. The wonderful thing about Sinclair's poems is that they are generous and invite you into their humble corners, where you see that her poems touch the world in all the ways you approach her poems — with affection, thoughtfulness, intimacy; with a tough regard; with a desire for magic and the fear of intruding upon it.

At first glance, the world is as it appears to be, solid, fixed, obvious, a chair here, a table there. But we miss how we are always imagining these tables and chairs into being. The light changes, the colour changes, the eye travels. I am looking at a dining-room table. I'm never able to quite see its entirety. I look at one corner, then across the surface, then at the nearest leg. When I try to conjure it in my mind's eye, I can't quite see it all. I'm assembling the pieces, but they're evanescent. One leg disappears as I bring forward the other. It belonged to my grandmother — domestic furniture belonged to women in those days. She died when I was five, and years later my aunt tells me how forlorn I looked on that day. I start to cry, and I'm astonished at my own tears. I did my homework on this table growing up. It is a faithful old dog. Sometimes when I peek in from the doorway, I see it wag its tail.

Sinclair quietly engages with all these uncertainties in perception. Let's examine a poem from her first book, *Secrets of Weather and Hope,* called "Red Pepper." The object is simple enough, and she begins with a description of it: "Forming in globular / convolutions, as though growth / were a disease, a patient / evolution toward even greater / deformity." Yes, the bulbous and creased twists of the red pepper lean toward the grotesque, and we feel it, sense its deformity. Yet the red pepper, of course, is simply following its normal growth pattern, as we can see in Sinclair's careful choice of the word "evolution," suggesting the long progress of natural selection that brought it to what it was before human cultivation. One of the ironies of the pepper is that humans have selected the traits that it expresses today.

So, if we think of the red pepper as a deformity, it is because what we want to see is the perfect circle, or globe, that is the beauty of Aristotelian proportion. We arrive at the pepper with a paradigm of perception that invokes ideas of perfection and deformity. Sinclair continues: "It emerges / from under the leaves thick / and warped as melted plastic, / its whole body apologetic: / *the sun is hot.*" Poetry is the art of associative thinking, and where there is associative thinking, similes and metaphors arrive like guests at a party. The earlier contemplative simile juxtaposing growth and disease is now replaced with the razor-sharp simile placing the pepper next to melted plastic.

Deformity is now made graphic. But it is just at this moment that the pepper starts to become human: it is "apologetic."

The second and third stanzas slowly develop an identity between the human and the pepper. In a deft manoeuvre, we are asked to put our hand on "it," which is followed by the note that it is the same size as a heart; but in the logic of metaphor, the hand recoils from the red pepper as it becomes a heart. By the third stanza the two have become indistinguishable. To touch is almost painful, but compelling because it is familiar. Experience has given the heart the "dents" and "twisted symmetry" inherent in the body of the red pepper. This provides the pathos of the concluding line, both astonishing and inevitable: "You can see how hard it has tried." What has it tried? It is the heart, of course; it has tried to love.

One might think that this is to personify, or even to anthropomorphize, but it is neither of these things. It is an epistemology, a denaturing roil of pathos, eros, metaphor, rhetoric, and embodiment. Humans confront the world, take hold of it, in a fundamental attitude of embarrassment or, in this poem, "apologetic," "abashed," "painful," and "familiar." As language, poetry pushes us toward the abstract, of thinking and emotion, and it is the object, the red pepper, that forces us to live in the body, for the body of the world is, as Wallace Stevens would have it, "wholly body, fluttering its empty sleeves." There are Sinclair poems more complex than this one by magnitudes, but the poems always have as their base the energies of this epistemology. I chose to look at this poem, for you can see how hard it has tried to make things appear as they are.

II
To Be Otherwise

"I, I, I. Abandoned mine shafts / descending to voiceless / tunnels," begins the poem "Sympathy," from Sinclair's second book, *Mortal Arguments*. Stark despair is uncommon in Sinclair's poetry, but when it appears, it is almost always voicing a failure to position the self ethically. "I, I, I" is the obsessive stutter of the ego, a cry for attention. The three *I*s look like mine shafts. They are a visual metaphor. The ego is the self, shouting its anguish and lost in the mine, but also it *is* the mine and its voiceless tunnels. Ultimately, the ego can only speak to itself, which is to be voiceless.

Prison is a common metaphor for the way the ego binds the self, and the window is the way through to the universe and its truths. In the ambiguity of Sinclair's image of the prison window, it is unclear whether one is breaking out of the prison of the ego or breaking into the space of a selfless self. The poem ends with a bleak metaphor in which one can bend back the bars but cannot squeeze through: "Denied access even to what / you most want: yourself, selfless." An ethics of intersubjectivity seems impossible.

Or so you might think, but Sinclair's poems ripple with multiple selves. Even in poems that do not have an obvious persona, poems about objects, or poems that observe others, such as *Breaker*'s "Pawel Laughing on the Beach," the speaker is not neutral — a pliable self is implied, changing as it is observing, learning from what it observes. Many poems read as autobiography, and in these poems, the self appears to withdraw but is, in fact, always present, the "Sue Sinclair" who lives in the moment of the poem. It is crucial in reading her poetry to pay close attention to pronouns, for they often carry the weight of how the self is posed and shaped by the other. "Photograph of My Mother as a Child *or* Invitation to the Wedding," from *The Drunken Lovely Bird*, is an engaging piece of family lore, but notice how it begins: "You wouldn't have told it this way, / but this is the story." Not "*I* wouldn't have," but "*you*." Who is this *you*? It is a pronoun that occurs frequently across all her collections, and it seems to have two valences: the singular *you* that is the self looking back at the *I*, and the *you* as other, which is any given reader. The ambiguous *you* is the invitation to be the "Sue Sinclair" of the poem, however intimate that might be. We might say that the "I, I, I" has been undermined.

In ethical thought, to be selfless is to serve others ahead of yourself, to be of service. Sinclair wishes for this, certainly, but she proposes the selfless self in more radical terms; to be selfless is not an ethical stance, but the ground for ethics itself. To be a waiting self, or even an idle self, is to be ready for an ethical encounter with the other. It is to say, *I am ready to be expressed and shaped by you even as I express myself.* Throughout Sinclair's poetry you can observe speakers seeking to find an ethical reserve in relation to the confusing world in which they find themselves, sometimes failing, sometimes awkward, sometimes blind, sometimes lashing out, but also occasionally rejoicing, loving, giving respect, and stepping forward. Ethics in philosophy can be very abstract, full of precepts, maxims, and logical propositions; and Sinclair is a philosopher by training, but her poetry is full of *people*, observed at work and play. Even mythical figures are reinvigorated as ordinary people. Readers are always encouraged and sometimes required to step into the position of the speaker and imagine themselves as other than they are. The poems are redolent with sympathy.

III
Something New under the Sun

Sinclair's poetry is profoundly ecocritical, but this is not obvious; indeed, many of the poems might be carelessly dismissed as "mere landscape." In the current climate, it is hard to imagine an innocent or naïve landscape poem, but Sinclair's landscapes do something we might call an epistemology of ecocritical thinking. This naturally follows from her explorations of the epistemology of perception and her positioning of the ethical subject. Each poem flickers through the ways we might offer ourselves to the natural world and the ways it offers itself to us. While ecocritical manifestos scattered throughout contemporary poetry do the easy work of reminding readers of the urgency they already know, Sinclair does the hard work of thinking through the new ways we need both to envision and to literally see the natural world if change is actually going to happen.

In "Breakwater," a poem from her fourth book, *Breaker*, Sinclair observes the building of a breakwater in her home province of Newfoundland and Labrador. On an island colloquially known as "The Rock," where people are intimately aware of the constant slap and grind of the North Atlantic, the piling of rock to create and maintain small harbours is fundamental to the imagination of place. This landscape is a space both literal and socially constructed. The poem's title is already based on a complex wordplay with the book's title. A breaker is an ocean wave that "breaks" when it collapses onto the shore, but the idea of a "breakwater" is to hold back the waves. Unbroken glacial erratics are lifted from the shore and placed on the breakwater, to shore up the breakwater, as it were. The wordplay mimics the perpetual exchange between ocean and rock, and so language is bedrock and bedrock a kind of language.

In this poem, as in so many in her oeuvre, the natural world answers and embodies human imagination, and Sinclair underscores that we cannot know the natural world as it is; every ecocritical utterance is framed by an act of perception that already implicates the human "view." In the first stanza of "Breakwater," the erratics are tinged with human characteristics: "Embarrassed, their awkward bodies / dangled in mid-air as though they had been / woken from sleep, taken unprepared." In the primal scene of embarrassment, our bodies and theirs laid bare, we find the human in the rock. There is a subtle allusion, though, to the way the rocks are far beyond the human, for the sleep from which they have been awoken is one of deep time, a geological time going back perhaps as far as the earliest iterations of life on earth. This exchange in the first stanza sets us up for the extraordinary second stanza:

> We were afraid of something they
> represented, their blank faces
> looking sombrely into the future,
> monuments to a mistake we had yet

to make, traces of something
we wanted to erase before it could exist,
We haven't eluded it. No better off,
we've forfeited consolation, won't know
where to go in our grief.

If, in the coming cataclysm of global warming and the injuries humans have wrought, we bring about a thorough devastation of life on this planet as it exists now, the mass extinction we appear to be in the middle of, remorse will be meaningless. The rock will provide no consolation, and we will have no place to go with our grief. Should this mass extinction include humans, rock, both product of and witness to the deep time of the past, will stare indifferently into a sombre future without us.

In her third collection, *The Drunken Lovely Bird*, Sinclair presents a painful portrait of exactly what a place of no consolation might look like. "Moratorium" describes an old fisherman after the cod fisheries have collapsed. The moratorium prohibited fishing for cod, a livelihood for generations of Newfoundlanders, in hopes the stocks would return. The portrait is of a desolate pain: "Old stories of codfish so plentiful you could / scoop them up. Hurts to remember / how good it was. The thought of the ocean / is an old nail hammered into his body, / rusted into him." The double remove is particularly striking: not the nostalgic, old, rubbed coin of "codfish so plentiful you could scoop them up," but now the tedious stories themselves, "so plentiful." Nothing to do but wait around to die. The poem concludes: "The sky shames him now. / He buries himself in his armchair. His life is a small boat / in which he is afraid to stand."

Heaven's Thieves, Sinclair's fifth and most recent collection, turns its attention to questions of hope, beauty, and spirituality. If we are in a world of hurt, is there something to ask for? At her most wry there is not much in any of these. Yet in a post-secular world, she can't help but turn questions of spirituality, hope, and beauty around in her head. One expects what humans have always proposed, that faith of some kind, even in an unknown, is the surety of hope and beauty. What's fascinating about Sinclair's meditations is that beauty is the surety of hope and faith. My reading of *Heaven's Thieves* — and where else but heaven could we steal, and steal away with, beauty — is that these impulses ultimately fail us, but perhaps they sustain us in an illusory way. Perhaps beauty is a beautiful illusion, and that is enough.

"Loving Pavlova" is the poem where these concerns receive the most thorough examination. The structure of the poem is unusual: two prose paragraphs, followed by a line or two of philosophical musing in italics, in four iterations. The prose paragraphs alternate between images and observations of the dancer Anna Pavlova, famous for her performances of *The Dying Swan*, a solo dance choreographed to *Le cygne*, a piece of about four minutes from Camille Saint-Saëns's *Le Carnaval des animaux*, which Pavlova had had commissioned for herself; and the "pale blue dot," the insignificant speck that is planet Earth in a photo taken by *Voyager 1* as it was leaving the solar system. Though seeming like an odd pairing, both share a precarious relation to the fragility of beauty, our desire for it, and our faith in its lie.

In part, Pavlova is the illusion on stage that performs a perfect, beautiful death that is applauded back into life, and the sacrifice behind the scenes, and even the ugliness, her "bad teeth — really terrible. Ruinous." And we come to her real death, when her breath is as short as the breathing after a performance, and she insists that her tutu, emblem of the fantasia of beauty she performed so many times, be laid out beside her.

What literally ties Pavlova with Voyager 1 is the idea of the photograph. Sinclair's own photo of Pavlova, in which the dancer is tiny, the size of Sinclair's thumb, is juxtaposed with the famous "pale blue dot" photo taken by Voyager 1. The photo of Pavlova articulates, despite its size, the detail of every feather and how the feathers are pinned to her shoulders, as if she alone must carry the shawl of beauty, while the "pale blue dot" has no detail at all, and is iconic for precisely that reason — it is the ultimate picture of the Earth, so remote as to invoke a longing, for home, for hope in a better world, for a speck of earthly beauty. Its meaning is, in part, imbued by the humans who made such a fantastical machine capable of taking the picture, but it is also in the way the pale blue dot drives a compulsion to reach out and touch it, experienced by scientists used to thinking about technical problems, from the first moment it was put up at the Jet Propulsion Laboratory. Carl Sagan originated the idea of taking the photo and first coined the phrase *pale blue dot*. In his famous speech he points to the blue dot and says, "That's us." He speaks of the carnage humans have inflicted on the planet and each other, but also of the possibilities of hope that come from seeing how small we are.

The philosophical reflections that punctuate the prose paragraphs turn on the question of beauty and truth. Sinclair begins with a question: *"Why not give in to beauty, consider its truth?"* The idea of giving in suggests a resistance, a thinking that beauty is a deflection from the truth. By the second italicized passage, beauty is a desire to see things better than they are, but also to see the best in them, which *"isn't a lie, or if a lie, only partly so."* In the third, the hope that Sinclair hangs on beauty, that we can't help but believe in, the one that draws us to the pale blue dot, is the smallest of white lies. At the end of the poem, beauty is not a lie; it is bound to the truth and remains for humans as *"just the most bearable part of the truth."*

Humans are something new under the sun, the only form of life, as far as we know, with enough memory to have consciousness, and enough consciousness to be aware of our own inevitable death, memory long enough to invoke the elegiac throughout our lives. We are capable of the most ingenious violence, including the most extraordinary violence to our planet. This violence is one kind of beauty, explored in "Exercise in Beauty No. 2," as alluring as the beauty of Pavlova: "I took a lighter to a seagull feather." But where is poetry in all of this? No one can deny the beauty of poetry even as it points at the most horrific things imaginable. Perhaps poetry is a breakwater, an arm extended to create a small harbour, a protection of beauty, for the time being.

IV
When Push Comes to Shove

In her new work, Sinclair continues the patient work of epistemology through close observation, but there is a new, more overt, political turn in her work. There are poems of pregnancy and motherhood that are exquisite but steely-eyed, asking questions of what is given and what is taken in the exchange between mother and child. Having a child is the breaking of choice into necessity, as she says in "Strange Heaven." A baby is born, but Sinclair critiques the prevailing ideology that affirms a woman's worth only in motherhood — an enveloping pressure felt, even now, by women who have decided not to have a child.

Frequently in these new poems, Sinclair questions the motives of the aesthetic. "To the Farmers Hand-Pollinating Pear Trees in Hanyuan County, China" invokes the lyric's reverence for a painterly scene of the pastoral and peasants performing the same work by hand passed on through the centuries. "It's not wrong — is it? — to see this as prayer, the chicken-feather wand, the jar of pollen round the neck, sacred objects both." This little piece of orientalism, so common in contemporary lyric, is exploded in the next stanza: "It's not wrong if (1) painstaking labour is synonymous with prayer, and (2) prayer may be performed for less than two dollars an hour."

Her politics hit closer to home in poems about the Sisson open-pit mine for tungsten and molybdenum proposed for central New Brunswick. In "The Nashwaak River" Sinclair uses the same technique as in "To the Farmers"; she begins with the lyric. "The river: it used to feel unstoppable. // What is beauty without the rush of blood, the promise it used to evoke?" This is followed immediately by a quotation from the *Sisson Project: Final Environmental Impact Report*: "The possibility of a structural failure of a TSF embankment is so unlikely that it cannot reasonably be considered a credible accident or malfunction, and thus is not considered further in this EIA Report." The Sisson literature casually points to the logging activity in this area for over a century with the suggestion that the mine is simply a continuation of long-accepted resource extraction. In her final line, Sinclair rebuts: "Stripped of trees, the banks are already crumbling."

The politics is constructed upon ways of knowing nature and human intersubjectivity, seen through the metaphors, the lyric intensity, the close observation, and the attention to the details of language in poetry. Aesthetics is often seen as a branch of philosophy, something studied by specialists in that area, but Sinclair's poems demonstrate that there must be an aesthetics of politics that is active in our relations with the world. Hitler thoroughly understood this, and the Nazis spent vast amounts of time on insignias, uniforms, art, architecture, and the choreography of marches, invoked recently, for example, at the Unite the Right rally in Charlottesville, Virginia, in 2017.

Sinclair explores this in the poem "Hey Nonny Nonny," where she uses the encounter of three young men practicing calisthenics in the park as the occasion for her thoughts on purity, beauty, aesthetics, and the politics of the "eerily *völkisch* return to nature." During the COVID-19 pandemic: "The gyms have closed / so they're back-to-the-land — beautiful / in their pursuit of health and strength / in this merry month of May / but alarmingly utopian looking, / suggestive of purist attempts to stamp out / dissent by way of just such beauty, / white skinned and forceful." There is immediate danger in the rise of neo-fascism and its Aryan aesthetics of "youngmanliness." Its counter-aesthetics is in exactly the kind of poetry Sinclair writes.

V

A Brief Summation

In this introduction I have moved from the epistemology of perception to the ethics of the self, to the ecocritical and its relation to beauty, and finally, to the aesthetics of politics and the politics that result. Now let me turn it around. Sinclair's poetry has always been political. There are the occasions when she guides her poems to an overt politics. But politics is somewhat empty rhetoric without the detailed and ongoing — just as history itself is ongoing — investigation and articulation of the epistemologies that have brought us to this point in history. Sinclair is one of our most significant nature poets, and her poems demonstrate that it is the close observation and engagement with landscape that informs ecocritical activism. A constant interrogation of ideas of beauty tells us much about what "ecocritical" means, and perhaps about what "nature" is. The complex uncertainty of ethics and positionings of the self tell us what kind of activism we should embrace. And in the recognition that what we perceive is always shimmering, shifting, and mutable, we understand that a fixed doctrine of politics is built on sand. I wish at this point that I could adduce the appropriate quotation from one of Sinclair's poems to express everything that needs to be said, but her poetry evades such simplicity. So, we offer *Almost Beauty: New and Selected Poems*, a collection that displays, from page to page, Sue Sinclair's evolving range of poetic thought.

NEW POEMS

The Prado

Afterward, I asked myself what I'd looked for.

Some faces, I thought. Faces of saints. Faces of lions. Faces of prophets. Faces of mothers. One face looking into another, perhaps.

The faces that look out from the frame the way I feel myself looking out from wherever consciousness lies.

The face of the servant holding the bloodstained nails removed from the cross, how he looks down, puzzled, from the ladder on which he's propped.

That's how I want to write. And then I want to look the way I've tried to write.

You can practice this at museums. I try meeting the eyes of those willing to meet mine, try to feel what it is to be willing. Poems, too, are practice: I am looking at you now — are you looking at me?

I want a world that is trustworthy. I want to lay the best version of my faults at your feet as you do the same for me.

I imagine Hieronymus Bosch watching us writhe and tear and eke our way toward the available pleasures: a ripe strawberry. A bird, a hand. A face.

If there is in me something worth being seen, let it look out at you from my face.

Let me try.

Let me try again.

Shall We Gather

The flood is not mine to suffer but only to dabble
my fingers in, skimming the rim of its shameless silvery waste,
touching the hem of its robe. It shines like grass,
like a grown-over dumpsite, holy, holy, holy. This is a new kind
of incarnation, pressing up against the houses, creating
new belief systems. The putrid scents that drifted through town
from what seemed like elsewhere now cling to our clothes.
Does every dawn radiate in some sense? For how long?
You can see it, the shift in theology; even the reflections
of the clouds have changed. A meniscus of light quivers around us,
barely holding itself together. The river's current reproduces itself
in the body as adrenalin. What has happened to us that immediacy
feels like an out-of-body experience? Let's pull our hands out
of the river, friend, no more gathering-at, not on this bank:
rebuilding isn't a twenty-first-century option.

Hey Nonny Nonny

Three young men in identical
navy T-shirts perform calisthenics
in the woods. Gymnastics rings are knotted
over a pine branch for pull-ups;
two men execute dated deep-knee
bends. The gyms have closed
so they're back-to-the-land — beautiful
in their pursuit of health and strength
in this merry month of May
but alarmingly utopian looking,
suggestive of purist attempts to stamp out
dissent by way of just such beauty,
white skinned and forceful.
The sun itself streams parental approval
over their shoulders as the ferns and
just-emerging Canada lilies pierce the litter:
why shouldn't they make the most
of the day, of their twenty-something prime?
The leopard frogs in the pond nearby
are thawing in the mud after a winter
spent in a near-death state,
frozen to the core. As they slowly
return to kinesthetic life, what might
they think of these fine specimens
of youngmanliness,
of this eerily *völkisch* return
to nature, of their diligent reps?
I haven't even mentioned the Adonis
butterflies, flashes of blue darting by,
opening and closing

their wings energetically,
empowered by the privilege of light.
It's partly the pandemic talking —
my fear of the purisms
that grow in such times, authoritarians
creeping out of chrysalides.
The young men have little to do with it —
they're packing up, *later, man.*
But how much delight and how much
dismay, that's what I'd like to know.
How can I tell and who do I ask.

The Peonies

They elbow their collective way past beauty — so essentially
plentiful, bullishly iterative, they encroach on the grotesque,
though beauty could be said to predict, even invite such a movement,
always at least a little too much of a good thing. Drenched with affect,
soaked through with a materiality that refuses to be marginalized,
this wilful self-occupation, this rallied congregation,
with its leaky canopy of perfume, has no control over the assembly
and demands none, allows the sensorium to be pushed to its nth
    degree,
sees exaggeration not as denial of reality but a way of displaying
one's commitment to it: the crowd has no permits and is loath to
    disperse.

Reprieve*

At first, I confused purity and authenticity.

I aimed true but ungodly high, didn't know what I was trying to do.

I could have died.

A person can try too hard, even if it's in their nature to try too hard.

In school lunches, I couldn't tolerate under or overripe fruit. Then I couldn't tolerate fruit at all, the scent, the sweat.

Synonyms for purity: tyranny, lack, forfeiture, immortality, safety, self-harm.

For authenticity? Home, I think, where home is any circumstance from which one doesn't flee — at least not willingly.

For years I pursued my heavenly self, its odourless trail. I had been determined to make it serenade me, yield its perfect measures.

There's no such thing as a lack of consequences.

I got sick, then I got better.

Every separation is a link. I don't quite believe that, but it feels closer to truth than it used to.

---

* The italicized line is from Simone Weil, *Gravity and Grace* (Routledge & Kegan Paul, 1952).

Pastoral

All day, the willow's leaky
faucet drips.

Flies crawl on the burlap bag
over the horse's head.

The barn's shadow lies across
the field like a farmer's suit
laid out on a bed.

The Nashwaak River*

The Sisson Mine project is a proposal to build one of the world's largest open-pit mines for tungsten and molybdenum in the heart of the upper Nashwaak River, near the village of Stanley, New Brunswick.

The river: it used to feel unstoppable.

What is beauty without the rush of blood, the promise it used to evoke?

"The possibility of a structural failure of a TSF embankment is so unlikely that it cannot reasonably be considered a credible accident or malfunction, and is thus not considered further in this EIA Report."

Thistles glint, molybdenum-like. Wild strawberries dangle from delicate trusses.

The water is bright as an eye; I feel like I could look into it, and it would know what I know about the Feds, the arsenic, the fluoride.

A middle-aged woman in flaw-concealing black swimsuit and white bathing cap wades up to her waist from the far bank.

Is there really such a thing as a core of self that can't be harmed, broken, broken into?

Uncannily calm, the flickering current.

Uncannily calm the ox-eyes, the vervain, the nightshade.

---

* Quoted lines are from Stantec Consulting, *Sisson Project: Final Environmental Impact Assessment Report*, February 2015, https://www2.gnb.ca/content/gnb/en/departments/elg/environmenv/content/environmental_impactassessment/sisson.html. "TSF" is an abbreviation of "tailings storage facility."

I consider the possibility of structural failure.

A credible accident: the damselfly perched on a stalk of timothy grass, shaggy with seed.

Before my eyes, beauty concedes, becomes a tactic, a way of putting things off.

At the foot of the maple a cluster of white *Pieris* butterflies sucks the salt from a patch of dog pee.

Come live with me and be my love...

Stripped of trees, the banks are already crumbling.

Tungsten Mine

Pity the filaments, those costly tongues.
The ore grade: 0.06%, a thimbleful in a tonne of rock,
hardly worth the effort. They know it, the filaments, ruminate
as they perform their tricks for us, summoning light
as if from the ether, as if it were a memory
we were forcing from them. They carry the burden
of their aggregate waste, of the tailings' passing semblance
of a pond, those doppelgänger-like fluids
that shine like real water. But there's no one for them
to tell, not really, and it's too late anyway —
that's a worst-moment thought, but it was
a worst-moment kind of place, the kind that naturally
leads to the sparing of details:
read what you can in the purposefully
matter-of-fact light cast into the room.

Overburden[*]

The land did not suffer, they reported, but a belief in suffering had never been among their articles of faith.

"Land" was a concession, though they didn't make concessions, so who can really tell.

They wanted us all to get along, shied away from conflict, were people pleasers at heart, betas, they confessed.

The squirrels chattered angrily at the excavators at first, but you know squirrels, always losing their shit about whatever.

The moose didn't bother to show up, and frankly we were glad not to have to contend with their droopy nostrils and tick-ridden skins.

It all happened outside town limits, one of those towns barely noticed by the capital as it breathes traffic into and out of its depreciating lung.

We usually tried not to think about it and pretty much succeeded. Did a dumped boulder ever appear in our dreams, just sitting there, not doing anything, in the middle of whatever we were actually trying to dream about?

If so, it wasn't a moment we wanted to recall.

The unburdening, they had promised, was just a change — like the changes any of us might undergo, quite naturally, on our way to adulthood. Later, their voices dropped so we had to lean in to hear: we knew, they said, what we were getting into.

---

[*] *Overburden* is a name for the layer of rock, soil and ecosystem that sits above and around an ore body.

Or no, they didn't say such a thing, not like that, and if they did, it certainly wasn't a threat. They wanted us to feel welcome to come to them with any concern.

There were tire tracks, which, they said, were a form of flattery.

There were trenches in rings, patterned like Parisian arrondissements.

There were paycheques for a while.

Then they left, and we were alone with the tailings ponds, their residual glitter repulsive to us.

They had replenished the shoreline with a handful of deteriorating warning signs.

Our one passive-aggressive act was to blot them out of the census for those years. That is, we performed an act of vengeance so perfect as to conform to their wishes exactly.

The Mine Speaks

Do not look upon my ugliness; it does no one any good.
Others have tried and failed, and there is no reason to believe
you may do more, though your kindness moves me,
it does. Perhaps the ferns will accomplish
some useful deed here, and the new grasses
that may come, perhaps then we will meet and exchange
the covert affections that pass between the looker
and the looked upon. For now, I have no such confidence.
You may, though, if it agrees with you, keep me
among your thoughts. And I will picture you
as if we were waiting together for a long-delayed train —
I would like to know you are there, on the opposite end
of the platform, straining toward that spot on the horizon
where a new body or new understanding of the body
just might reveal itself. I fear, though, that I will be forgotten.
Which is almost enough to push me to court your gaze,
despite the shudder the thought engenders.
But no, I cannot bear it. Do, I implore you, go —
let enough time pass and I will hope someday to greet you
as if in the old way, though we will both know
that everything, everything has changed.
Let that, my friend, be the ground upon which we meet.

Tokens*

Oh daffodils, "oh bright assembled matter,"
cruelly fringed, yellow
and odourless,
                forgive me. How have I taken you
to be less real than you are, mere cultivars
deprived of subjectivity? Even now,
as you flash upon my inward eye,
I most recall the lack
on which your excess seems to draw,
not even the ghost of a scent straying
among you, tickling your stiff collars. I have pitied you
the evolutionary advantage
of your good looks — endless scentless replicas
propagated ad nauseum. I have looked at you as if
you were no more than a poorly
executed plan on which no outcome
now depends.
                "How very many names
you have when you are loved" — I'm sorry
not to have named you till now, to have been so sparing
with my love. I didn't think I was the kind
to scapegoat:
                why was this so hard for me to see?
Oh daffodils, please,
be the warrant for my second effort —

---

* Quoted lines are from poems in Lisa Fishman's *The Happiness Experiment* (Ahsahta Press, 2007).

I'm rallying,
          I'm running a finger along your green spines.
I'll do better — I'm tying a knot in this afternoon
sunlight
      as a reminder: from now on my eyes,
my blood, my nerves will leap
at your bidding.

Ampersand

It's the Hogarthian curve that gets me,
the "line of grace." It's not beautiful in a cool,
breaking-the-golden-rule-of-proportion kind of way,
but mathematical perfection is a real thing —
not the only thing, but one or two marvels
among the rest. See how after the ampersand crosses
itself, it opens? If I could make that gesture
a thousand times a day, I might be a better everything
to everyone, myself included. I don't deny
the possible deceptions: a lyric flourish
briefly defying time, looping the loop,
insisting on respite from history
& its attendant pains. It pretends to move
things along but instead makes pause,
& I'm not fool enough to believe history's struggle
is done, but am perhaps fool enough sometimes
to dream of that end. The ampersand sympathizes;
it was once a letter, twenty-seventh in the alphabet.
Then it drifted, away & away & away
to wherever beauty makes landfall,
& I lean into the curve, somehow think I can follow —
as though Pythagoras himself were urging me on,
gesturing to the false horizon between here and heaven,
calling this beggar to *ride, ride, ride* as far as I can
before hunger drives me home.

Exposé

Too late: the oyster
mushroom I cull from its roost
in a local maple is ravished
by worms making a famished lace
of its insides, hideous
and beautiful by turns —
like the famous duck-rabbit,
which won't hold still, resolve itself
into a single aspect, come to a
respectable conclusion.
The mushroom is a sign
of the maple's decline, the sign itself
now succumbing to death's
crusade against the very idea
of stability — folding
life inside life with a Möbius
twist, making agents
of the small *o*'s of the worms'
appetitive mouths. Beyond
the irony of the death feeder's
own demise is this writhing,
this lacing and unlacing of selves,
apparent for a moment
in the saprophytic flesh
that finds its twin in the worm
who chews on its fan-like
gills, renovates its underside.
Here, in rare microcosm,
the thread of life
pursuing itself from one form
to another, the restless
cycling of nutrients through all
who offer it passage.

It Could Happen to Anyone[*]

Of the boletes, only some are edible.
Yet I seem to crave the evil twins, the toxic
satisfactions of their tell:

rupture the skins, break the seal,
and in seconds they turn the blue
of a medieval Mary's robes as she looks up

to hear of her strange fate —
a colour so unnatural, a conversion so quick
and complete as to seem miraculous,

which is to say a little sickening.
Sometimes I think I want it,
"the glorious suture" mending skepticism,

but what good would that do
when uncertainty suits me so well?
This blue makes me cringe,

disrupts truth, leaches out the doubt
I'd always imagined as clinging
in earnest symbiosis to the real.

Is it a vision, the unearthly colour rising
through the flesh? Is nausea the sign
that vision is occurring?

---

[*] "The glorious suture" is a phrase from Lisa Robertson's poem "Toxins," *3 Summers* (Coach House Books, 2016).

And what would it mean to be granted
such a thing, even its parody
if that's all skepticism will allow?

I cup the bolete's emergent strangeness
and will it to continue, the feeling
of right-before-my-eyes. I imagine this

is what being with God is like for true
believers: wondering how far to presume,
how to approach, what intimacy might

come of it: right there, in my palm,
though I'm just a dilletante,
a dabbler. Maybe next time

I'll have learned to be properly
transfixed — maybe I won't be the one
who looks away first.

Sex Ed Just Got Weirder[*]

Don't be fooled: sure, fungi perform standard-issue
reproductive tricks, scattering spores — ho-hum —
but also this other flagrant thing, hyphae fusing
in the dirt web, mycelia interlacing, passing genetic
material across species, trading even nuclei,
so that what it is to begin or end, to be one thing or another
gets woozy: taxonomies blur, genetic trees branch off the page
and into three dimensions, reach into my gut to ask
who am I anyway, what tracts I think I have
that won't be breached, what yeast-less skin, bacteria-free
nasal passages, what mind that doesn't inhale
thought? School me, fungi, in your queer habits,
procreating by downward thrust and outward
sprawl, your cross-species joie de vivre submitting
one more sorites paradox, showing how hard it really is
to know x's from y's, you from me, both of us from
the persistent breaching of thresholds, elastic couplings,
this benign philandering, this category creep —

---

[*] This poem owes a debt to Merlin Sheldrake's conversation with Robert Macfarlane in the latter's *Underland: A Deep Time Journey* (Penguin, 2019).

Thoughts and Prayers
after David Zsako's work of the same name

Can you even stand to look at me? Bristling
with handguns, sceptred by AK-47s —
I'm the survivor, the last of my familiars;
I'm the one who makes it out alive
because I don't give a shit,
because I thrive on neglect, feed on stale cliché.
Come on, assholes, try to take me out, I dare you —
shoot me up, put another bullet in my chest
and watch my heart get redder, more vainglorious —
see me dance, hear me screech, watch me explode,
expand, grow fruitful and multiply:
geranium, zinnia, rose, petals all plucked.
You think you're better than me, with your
half-assed prayers and Second Amendment fetishes?
I was summoned, don't deny it, conjured
to fill a void. *Yippee-kay-ai, motherfuckers.* It's on.

Birth of Mars

Some days the sun rises with a lean
and hungry look,
blazing, reading to devour us.
As though while we slept,
it took up arms
in a war in a desert
on the other side of the world.
Now it's back, still furious,
the taste of blood in its mouth —
doesn't recognize us,
looks at us as though we
were the enemy,
or as though the enemy
were hiding inside us.
It glares at the garbage trucks,
the flat-footed pigeons,
the traffic lights that keep
changing colour,
betraying themselves.
It glares and glares.
Because maybe this *is* the desert,
the streets heaped with bodies
we can't see. It could be
that we're still waking up
and will momentarily find ourselves
in the midst of a war
we haven't named yet,
afraid of what will happen
if we do.

Ultrasound

A corona of rays opens downward —
the way sunlight does when, swimming underwater,
you look up. The lost idea of God fits briefly
back into the hand.

Something, anyway, makes us feel that
our baby, or at least her image on the screen,
has been blessed, maybe not even on purpose.

She seems caught in a glow we're barely privy to,
peering at the staticky black-and-white dream
of her habitat. Which isn't to say her life — *life!* —
will mean any more or less,

just that for the moment, in the tiny Eden
of the womb, as she grows her very own
feet, hands, heart and lungs, she seems basked
in whatever that downpour of light is.

Service

I'm waiting for my life to change utterly.
This will happen: my belly swells
like a sail; the calm is involuntary,
a navigational trick as we steer past the last
buoy. I don't know who I'll be afterward,
distant twin to whom all I'll have to give
is who I am now. I wonder what use
I'll be, how she'll put me to work, servant
in the great house of her motherhood.
I wonder what her child will know of me
and what thoughts I have now that will rise
to run the bath, warm the room, then dim
the light, sending them both to dreaming.
I wonder what thoughts those thoughts
will have then, standing by the window,
wind gathering in the trees,
what new selves they may devise
as these strangers sleep.

Strange Heaven

A baby in the womb will strip its mother's bones, teeth,
blood. She will mine iron, enamel, potassium,
vitamins A through E. Which means my body
is not my own — only what's left over belongs to me;
I've become the scavenger. For though they call us one,
we are rather a rhymed two, and the shared syllable
may become silent — sterile — in the first instance.

I don't begrudge her the nutrients she craves,
but at times I do wish it otherwise, our being joined
in this uneven way. I take supplements
so there's no deficit — but I wish I could choose,
could really *give* her what she needs.

Choice, however, may be what's given up in the bearing
of a child, that one choice so utter, so thorough, it blasts
through all other choices to the never-before-visited
far side of the mountain. A place where necessity rules,
where all has been decided though the struggle isn't done,
and the light is crisp and clear in a way I'd never dreamed.

The Washing Place*

It wasn't so much the birth
as the days that followed. Remember
Odysseus before Nausikaa found him?
Before he could scrape the *scurf of brine*
from his shoulders? When he staggered
from the river, unsteady of foot
and uneasy of mind? It was like that,

and it went on like that
for some time. Lorazepam,
bitter under the tongue. Nausikaa
was sent to him by the gods,
but he was afraid of the girls' voices
he heard in the trees, and at first
did not know how to speak.

No more did I. Even if there were a word
for what had happened, the salt had torn
it from my throat. I pressed on.
What choice? I too heard the voices
in the trees, and like Odysseus, unclothed,
crusted with dry spray, I finally spoke:
I am at your knees, O queen, have pity.

---

* Italicized lines are borrowed from Richmond Lattimore's translation of *The Odyssey* (Harper Perennial Modern Classics, 2007).

Long Haul

Samson's bees hived themselves in the carcass of a lion.

Strange carcass this, the cavernous rumbling trailer dragged down the American highway, pollinators ready to hand, stacked in the darkness, sent to groom the fields.

If I told you that you could be endlessly happy, what kind of field would you imagine, what kind of release?

The engine drone vibrates endlessly through their bodies — but that could be a form of happiness for all I know. For all I know they dream of it.

Crossing the continent to conduct the rites of spring after the locals have died.

The Ancient Greek *nek* = *death* + *tar* = *overcome* yields *nectar*. The blossoms hoard this irony till the trucks arrive and disgorge the bees.

Industry darlings, they stumble too soon into the thin light of early January, spill into the almond grove, milk the blossoms blearily, fumble through the pink haze.

This isn't the first time I've mistaken idiom for truth.

In the old days families told the bees about death or disruption in the house, whispered the news into the hive's confessional. Poor bees: the house is so far gone now, I don't know how we'll ever speak of it.

They suck *death-overcome* into their weak bodies, as if making it true, as if a new economy will spring effortlessly from the ruins.

Reach your hand up as if to grasp some fruit, a gesture that can now only be posed as a question.

A hum in the orchard like a veil, like a thought spreading across a mind, almost convincing…

To the Farmers Hand-Pollinating Pear Trees in Hanyuan County, China*

It's not wrong — is it? — to see this as prayer, the chicken-feather wand, the jar of pollen round the neck, sacred objects both.

It's not wrong if (1) painstaking labour is synonymous with prayer, and (2) prayer may be performed for less than two dollars an hour.

Whose ambition was this?

Tumult, weeping, many new ghosts.

Labourers pick their way through the crowns of trees, cheaper to rent than bees, bodies thicker than the trunks they cling to, defying a sense of just proportion.

Spring has always been the season of awkward rites, but this year my heart skips a beat: what further sleight of hand will be called for? What feats of mimesis?

Everywhere people speak in whispers, understudies running rushed lines.

A labourer reaches up a hand to pluck an invisible bee from her hair.

The law of diminishing returns echoes through the orchard.

What day, what day, can I go home?

---

* Italicized lines are from Tang Dynasty poet Du Fu.

The Most Important Room in the World*

The gift no one wants, rows of ugly plastic storage containers, fluorescent lighting, steel doors.

The fusion of exemplary international cooperation and a queasy stomach, of the Scouting motto and a mountain, of prophesy and the seeds of clover, rye, wheat, spelt, dill, pumpkin, squash, spinach, barley, sorghum, bean...

Breathe the cold in the room.

A pragmatism that goes so deep it acquires a frisson of transcendence, hoarfrost on the tunnel walls.

Deep under the mountain, therefore mythical.

The opposite of a tomb — or is it?

An empty space where Aleppo should be, the local holdings destroyed in the war, a first withdrawal.

My archetypes feel a little too close for comfort.

Outside, Norwegians fight over whether to probe for more oil.

Inside, ice glitters indifferently.

---

* This room is the Svalbard Global Seed Vault, housed inside a mountain in the Norwegian archipelago of Svalbard. It contains more than 500,000 species of seeds from all over the world and has been built to withstand a variety of disasters. "The most important room in the world" is a phrase coined by the scientists who work there (https://www.rnz.co.nz/news/world/331227/ice-melt-affects-world-s-most-important-room). The words *the gift no one wants* are by Dyveke Sanne, the Norwegian artist who created the mirrored work *Perpetual Repercussion* (2007) which is affixed to the front of the vault. https://believermag.com/an-interview-dyveke-sanne/.

This is how we try to strip ourselves of contingency and how contingency sticks its foot in the door.*

It's why tourists want to visit and why they're not allowed:

promises we can't keep, histories we can't undo, ambitions more capacious than even 150,000 species of rice can conceive.

---

* The permafrost gave way in 2017, flooding the vault's entranceway.

SECRETS OF WEATHER & HOPE
(2001)

The Pitcher

Unafraid of the dangers
of perspective, of distance,
round as a fruit, sure
of its proportions,
it confides in us its secret:
an inch tall, an inch around,
dainty lip and handle
ready to pour.

You want to hold it in your hand
because it fits, and makes you believe
in a place as small and certain
as that, like the way we remember
childhood
          through a keyhole:
our tiny mother,
tiny father, the tiny bed
in which we slept. Did we dream?
We did not. The sun rose
again and again, digging up the day.
Endlessly we began. Our cheeks were rosy.
We cried tiny tears.

The pitcher shines, the persuasive
curve of its body leads you
into recollection. So small
there's no room for doubt.
But what doubt did you have? Some things
you never quite forgot, and some
you always believed were true.

Green Pepper

Glossy as a photograph, the bent
circumference catching
the light on its rim. Like a car's
dented fender, the owner desperate
to assess the damage, unable
to say, like the sun, *it can't*
be helped.

Conspicuous and irregular
all its life, born
with its eyes shut tight,
as though there really were a collision
it was trying to avoid. But it hasn't
happened yet—there is only
the impact of light: it has never

been in love, never drifted apart,
never fantasized about another
fragrant vegetable, never
been flattered, never been denied,
never wanted more than it has.
A life governed by absence:

the gleam of white
on its hollow body.

Red Pepper

Forming in globular
convolutions, as though growth
were a disease, a patient
evolution toward even greater
deformity. It emerges
from under the leaves thick
and warped as melted plastic,
its whole body apologetic:
the sun is hot.

Put your hand on it. The size
of your heart. Which may look
like this, abashed perhaps,
growing in ways you never
predicted.

It is almost painful
to touch, but you can't help
yourself. It's so familiar.
The dents. The twisted symmetry.
You can see how hard it has tried.

Upstream

Pouring over the weir, the river
is time reversing. The trout that flash
silver out of the water are splitting
seconds, infinitely, until the fragments
are so small you can't see them, invisible
flicks of light from their tails.

We aren't prepared for how myopic
they are, nosing at the falls, looking for a way
in. A leap, we say, expecting
a beginning and an end, but as long
as they hang there they are not made
of time. They do fall back, but
however briefly, the moment opens
up for them and they pass through,
even those who miss the mark
entirely — those perfect, useless arches.

Lilies

I

The callas, stylish
as the waved hair of women
who do lunch, picking at shrimp
over white tablecloths.
They leave the tails on the edge
of their plates, implying
that they have done this before, many times,
and don't even think of them
as tails anymore. It's a matter
of decorum, a neat snip
of the teeth. The waiter removes the plates.

II

That desire both
to be touched and not to be touched
quite yet. Inchoate even as they turn
their heads, hoping to be seen. They remind
you of adolescents, a single whorl
curled over at the edges, revealing
just enough to make you want
a way in, while it carries you around
itself, abandons you on the periphery.
You lose sight of where you are,
where you want to go; there is nothing
but this beginning.

III

Napkins drape across
the women's laps: the centre crease
is still visible, hinting
at the immaculate, at how quickly
they could be refolded and how clean
they will always be — so they think, and go on
thinking even after the women dab their lips
and go. All the women leave them like this,
carelessly crumpled. They have learned
that to remark on anything is to draw attention
from themselves. There is no mystery
to this; the flowers on the table
have figured it out: they won't tell you
anything you want to know.

André Kertész

about the light all
I can say is how it surfaces,
                            makes bare,
how nothing knows itself, the tulip
in its vase, opening,
        the railing which leads neither
up nor down but waits,
drowsy;
things are like this sometimes, indoors,
mid-afternoon,
                    every lit form proposes
not just the doing but the falling
into doing
           — ah, so it has happened
at last, the tulip,
            marooned
in its own vastness, complicates nothing

Lyric Strain

The hum of bees. How it unnerves us: we tremble
when a tree branch bends too low. The din
of traffic is almost more bearable than the garden
where a hungering quiet erupts from the roots,
cell by vivid cell.

A bee hovers near, quivers in the shadow
of the ear. We stiffen, scared it might drop
inside and set our bones ringing. The sound is after all
not too large but too small: a resonance our skulls
can't bear. What we feared wasn't the great brightness
but the minute trembling
of tiny hairs, that shiver of recognition.

Red and Orange Streak by Georgia O'Keeffe

If everything really did begin
as light. Then slowly filled the need
for flesh, for sweetness of bearing.

Oranges, pears, green apples
leaching inward, bleeding
internally. Firming up.

If a nectarine grew
from the outside in, it would look
like this. Fist of light
moulded onto darkness, darkness
like a last. Red hills in the distance.

Yellow accumulating weight
becomes orange. The belly of fruit
ripens: let us not forget then

the shrinking darkness, the hand
on the back of its neck, forcing it
down. Bullied into the centre
it crouches in a shrivelled
almond. Think of its frustration
when you bite in, interrupt
the meditation —
a nectarine concentrated
on compactness. On the face of it
there seems to be no thought
more pressing than the sky
but it has bled itself into being
and nothing wells up inside it
and nothing wills itself to grow.

Toronto Skyline

Nothing to cast a shadow
up there, buildings pale
and glittering, fascinated
by themselves and a little
ashamed. Far back in their minds
they know they have arrived empty-handed
but pretend they're not yet
where they want to be, wherever
that is. Sometimes, watching a pair
of starlings swoop and duck, they almost
admit it, give in to doubt. A kind of vertigo.
It's the heat, we say, that makes them
waver, and they ignore it too, wait
for it to pass. Be taller,
they say to themselves,
be taller, because that is the only way
they know how to think.

Stratus

They come as close
to us as sleep, leaving
heaven behind. Only the palest halo
stays around the sun —
                              a reminder.
If we were made of water
we might hover as they do, might be
as luminous. But they know
something of weight, an earthly
memory. You are tired
for no reason. You aren't really sure
you are awake. You feel far from home.

Cirrus

To look up
all that distance
is to anchor yourself
more firmly to the ground.
It reveals the throat, curved
like a spoon. There, your heartbeat,
faintly visible. The less you
have the more it shows. Your face.
Your chin.

Wispy clouds, threadbare, traces
of things which have passed
effortlessly, without concern.
You look up through icy shades
of blue: too high for memory.
Too high for rain. Nothing so remote
on Earth. The coldest, thinnest
part of you wants
to be up there, stillborn.

Cirrus Radiatus
Radiatus have long, parallel streamers of relatively similar size that appear to converge toward the horizon.
  — National Audubon Society Field Guide to North American Weather

It makes you believe
you have come from somewhere,
let's call it heaven: a kind
of convergence, a distance impossible
to breach. Only the clouds
bring it near: perspective, a trick
of the light, infinity
a point on the horizon.
                        Now we're sure
we can find our way and agree
to meet there, in the garden
we remember from the time before.
We will wait forever
if we have to, pluck apples
from trees, shuffle our feet
like angels do.

Stratocumulus Undulatus

How the light cuts
through the atmosphere, falling
through dust, dust, dust.
In the time it takes
to reach the Earth, someone dies.

The clouds barely notice.
They think of the dead, the dying,
no more than of the light,
which slips through unremarked.
They have their own concerns:
soon it will be time to rain again.
They gather up water. They murmur.

The places where the dead
used to eat, sleep, love are like that space
between earth and sky. An empty room.
The mourners, looking up, see nothing.
Blind even when they shade
their eyes. Although the light opens
as it nears the Earth, breaking a little
to fall on them more gently, they still
don't understand. They see only the rain
that hasn't yet come — that and the light like a prism
in its strict cut, dividing, dividing.
They cringe as though it were an incision
in the heart, not the sky. They look down.
If only it had arrived sooner.
The light, not the rain.
It doesn't matter now when
it rains.

Domestic Habits

The peculiar sadness when we watch animals
dream — does it awaken in us a travel
weariness, like the stars, part of that
distance, names silting
around our shoulders?

They are almost more familiar
asleep — a twitch, a low mutter
so much like worry you think
even they can't refuse insistent
thoughts, repetition — as if this
were something they didn't want
to admit: that they could easily
be like us. Though there's no proving it,
you are willing and fall for it. And just
when you're sure is when it becomes
hardest to bear:
                    that the hour changes
as they sleep, and when they wake up
they don't know what's happened
any more than we do.

Springtime

The day has given up trying to be
anything in particular, imagines itself
in another place and almost believes it.
The clouds change shape quickly. They don't see
we can't keep up, how much slower
our hearts are. On a day like this
all you can do is keep pace with yourself.
You might be tired. So might everything else.

The flowers coming up in the gardens
open slowly, resistant to change. Drops
of water cling to the crocuses, the white petals
like a swan's oiled feathers. You feel sorry
for them, forget they know places
no one else goes. This memory is strongest
when they are open widest; they can disappear
just by thinking about it.

Behind a second-storey window a man
steps back from the light; shadows
fall over him like a hand
over a face. But it's just the clouds
reflected in the glass. It would never have occurred
to them to vanish. They know nothing will ever
be quite the same again. The sky meets your eyes
knowing next time it will reveal
as much and as little.

The Scent of Wolf Willow

Like honey
and nutmeg, fresh
baked cake with an extra ingredient
that threatens to drive you
wild with nostalgia:

you think of bees, a cloud
humming all around
without touching you, of kitchens
gone wild, gone native:
                              imagine
opening a cupboard
full of silver leaves,

imagine walking into your kitchen
to find it had vanished:

tarnished cutlery
spread on the lawn for days
afterward,

the fridge lying
under a tree, licking itself
clean.

Wolf willow: whistle
and it will not come; its tiny flowers
pretend not to hear; hidden in the cleft
between leaf and branch, they close
their eyes, hoping you will go
so they can go on remembering her,

the one they want,
the one who isn't home yet.

Easy enough to imagine
she won't come: the scent
is heavy, sinks quickly under
its own weight, more dense
than anything visible.

March

The car, cooling, ticks
like a cricket. Left
to itself it tries to forget
speed, come to grips with where
it wishes it came from: the green
middle of nowhere. At times
like this, a spring thaw,
all of us marooned on curbs
begin to think this way.

It pretends not to see itself
in puddles. Ignores chrome
and polish and thinks of a place
far away, a place so small
you could hold it in your palm, so complete
it could only have been imagined.
Ask your mother: there was never
a Sunday drive, no aunt or uncle
in the country. But what are you to do
when even the car remembers the green
sides of the road, the bright air,
how its pistons purred?
It is entirely convinced: as the heat
dissipates it feels its body
shrink and almost believes
it's going back.

Grazing

The prairie lies belly up
in the sun, running
no risks: it has nothing more
to give up, nothing left to say.
It flourishes, literal, complete,
and doesn't resist the light:
you have travelled far, so have we all.
The flanks of the cattle shine
as they wander, heads down,
outcasts. There is no place
like home and it's useless
to search. No one could dream
anything stranger than belonging,
a horizon like this doesn't
allow for it. But it's as close
as you can get:
                the grass
laying itself out, the distance,
the stubborn light, the cows
flicking their tails.

Departure

Sometimes, autumn reveals the inward
light of things we call *glowing*.
A handful of red maple leaves.
A light that doesn't exceed itself
and has something to do

with departure. Think of a church,
the long, slow, sad colours, the way
they linger, miles from the sun, with no thought
of lingering. Again the red leaves.

Lay them on a table.
The dead have come back
to haunt the surface of the wood.
They can see themselves in the polish,
appear and disappear, something more than
and less than a face.

At the end of everything, you think,
there is this — this quickness,
this vanishing, this brilliance. The unseen
glimmer that bound it all together
escapes and is forgiven.

And everyone knows that forgiveness
gives off light, that healing
is the next thing to fire. It calls you
as it goes. You lay your
hand on the table.

MORTAL ARGUMENTS
(2003)

Birthday

Light dumped on our heads,
we become heaven's compost. Our thoughts,
like insects, chew through eternity's lost
causes, hours and days, time's least
digestible fibres. We take in what heaven can't
or won't put up with: living and dying,
the incomplete virtues of strength and weakness. It's not true
there is no fear in heaven: the gods keep
watch over us, are afraid of the losses
we hold, afraid to die. They don't trust
their own endlessness. You are the natural outcome
of immortality's inability to conceive.
The one thing it can't bear, which is why it needs you.

Prime

Dragonflies hover in tandem, glued
together at the ends
like the trees reflected in the pond, everything
in pairs,
    multiple,
        lily pads
rucked up against
each other, some lifted
from the water
like heroes carried home
on shoulders: frogs
ping like rubber bands,

the buzz, the glitter, flashbulbs
popping, so this
is where media was born,

its meaning asway
in the lushness of place,
full of ears, alert:

the world sits up, attentive,
listens to the story of itself from
beginning to end,

applauds wildly.

Vacation

The ocean roams
like a stray dog, whose name

no one knows, who's been
coming around so long

we don't bother guessing.
We lean back into the tired joints

of beach chairs and imagine our lives
as white lies. Waves

roll on the sand, and it's again
the dog, who won't tell

where his bone is buried. We don't care.
Two weeks go by, and only when

we're leaving, watching from the train,
do we know what we came for: to look back

at the shining sand, the ocean
stretched out under the sky. The shore,

as we go, lies open,
broken locket, weak hinge.

Witness I

Light says we should redistribute
the wealth, touches every surface. Its argument
is your own mortality: *is* becomes *ought*.

Children in the glassed-in pool
learn to swim, snapping their legs together
like mousetraps. Under your very nose, a thing becomes itself
by changing into another. The struggle
illuminates your own purposes:
never more than today

have you wanted to save the world, which means
moving as slowly as you can, as if life were a hive of bees
you dare not disturb. The greater good
is all around, buzzes as you look down at the pool,
the water aquamarine.

Springtime

The maples woo the car, its hood covered in pollen.

Nature attempts the impossible yet again, the only way it knows of coping with a dead end.

Longing wants to fuse with use.

What's a white Volvo to do? Without genetics, without family or anyone to follow it home.

Pollen under the windshield wipers, in all the intimate corners.

It's pure engine, can't think except in the past tense of fossil fuels.

Who's to say nature can't turn it into something more? There's no better time or place.

If there's any more luck in the world, let it find its way here.

Paddling

The shine, the square of light on every leaf,
lilies, more leaves, the *V* of the canoe in the water: gateway
to nowhere, the beginning of imagining you aren't.

Fear of profusion: where things are few, they seem
necessary. The trees and their thousand leaves massed
on the verge of disappearance.

Light clamps onto us; we'll have to skin ourselves
to be rid of it. Paddles dip in the water, dip and pretend
they don't know what goes on, don't see the world vanishing.

In the mind's mud, nothingness spawns. Where time becomes less
pressing, we feel its depth. The world is burnished: trees, bark, skin
going up in flame. The gods are not what you hoped they would be.

The sun, taking us all down with it.
Heedless, the ten thousand things.

Witness II

Beauty on the pedestal of itself. An enigma whose
question is its own being, whose answer
is also being. The future a deal it never makes. We empty ourselves
of desire, lay it down as we lay down weapons.

Grief is not something to be swallowed
but a faint halo around the living, a glow. Beauty, though,
has none, walks outside at night, alone: the elocution of the stars,
unpronounceable, perfect syllables. God encrypted
in the world.

The house grows smaller at night, trying
to lose itself in thought. We listen
to the sibilance of the refrigerator keeping time. Light
through the window, the stars shedding their skins.
Beauty even in beauty, when it's easiest to forget.

Roses

Not because it is sufficient, but because
we subsist on light, and what doesn't
cry out to be noticed? There's something here
you might recognize, but you're not sure; still, you're willing
to risk it: the loss is of everything, seen and unseen,
the before and the after. It doesn't depend on you,
but you move toward it. Because as long as there's a moment
here or there, why not arrange a few roses
in a jar, give thought to their listlessness, how they gather
the room about them yet think nothing of it, how each
thorn persists, how they have made a purpose
of holding still? Then you remember
the necessary and sufficient. This isn't it,
but you don't know where else to begin.

Dreamlife of Houses

Darkness persists even as you waken.

Your sheets like the skin of another animal, odourless.

An ache in your limbs: you slept too little.

Close your eyes, watch your dreams disappear into the distance. The vanishing point in your psyche.

Downstairs, the table hovers on the sill of the next day, its surface bare as if free of thought. Things still their pale, animal selves.

Like the rim of a falls where everything waits, about to plunge.

Your heart races.

Flick the switch, and light drops from the ceiling like a bird, stunned. Forgets to spread its wings.

Chairs sit in halos of shadow.

It's still dark. The ladder has disappeared: the night a wall you can't climb.

Witness III

The roses, at their most adjectival,
donate themselves to charity, subside,
abstain from their own majesty.
They are the linings of themselves,
softly receive nothing,
no tribute but their own being.

The day available as a flower: take me.
Only so much time, the afternoon succoured
by its own short-lived hopes,
wanting to be everything to everyone.

A spider spins a web simply to show
there is a perfect fit between all things.
The space between the porch and the rosebush
requires no adjustment. Between the rose
and its corollaries: earth, light.

Loose and heavy, the day's drowsiness
catches up to us: sleep takes us in
like a lungful of air. Under the arch
of the porch, nothing moves.

Cityscape

The narrow hips of the streets.

Business an empty pedestal.

In the municipal gardens roses clamber up, intent on solitude. Architecture, a pressure to live up to.

Watching sunsets sideways, vertical horizons at the end of day.

The city needs its failures, a measure of despair.

A childhood lisp becomes meaningless. The fear of innocence: carry yourself as if you've always known.

Buildings, torn down, leave their silhouettes on adjoining walls like ghosts.

The injured outlive us.

Love Poem II

The aspen roll back the whites
of their eyes, panicked. Winds
coming in from the North.

First snow
and I still haven't
kissed you.

The neighbours' bedsheets
on the line, the privacy
of inner life everywhere now.
Bare trees, naked lawn.

Waking up to a room
where light beats its wings
like a trapped bird.

The thin hum of phone lines:
your voice is clearer in the cold.

Wickaninnish

The litter of splintered wood
at the top of the beach, the silver edge
time leaves on things. The past,
and the moment when it shines a little.
From here it seems farther than ten miles
to the horizon, but they say
that's as far as you see. The sun
goes down and the logs take it to heart,
an orange glow. Illegible
rings in the wood: you are too young
to fully grasp the languages
in what you see. Concentrate,
and a glimmer of purpose may reveal itself,
but the unknown will still seek you,
laying its tinder inside you. The sun is stronger
than any of us. The logs, spread on the shore,
allow themselves to go blind.
They aren't afraid of fire.

Poem

The poem wants to be an extra bone
in the body. Lonely,
it wants the day to come back for it:
a jacket left at the coat check,
the dance floor deserted.

There is no wisdom in the poem,
but it repeats its small life as many times
as we ask. The poem is everybody's
mother, remembering what can't be found,
remembering who you are, remembering
what hasn't even happened yet.

Love Poem IV

The sun slaps itself
on the wall like a fresh coat of paint.
Awake, we listen to each other
breathe. The fragility of time,
its uncertainties. Handed down
generation to generation, like family heirlooms:
our consciousness, our waking hours. The morning
light perjures itself, says we have more time
than we know what to do with.
You turn to me: sometimes the soul
wants to be all windows.

Days in Between II

The long afternoon — a child wanting to be lifted and carried, heavier than we thought.

The trauma of brightness.

The traffic is tired, can't find its destination.

It slows, wilts.

We've stopped on the shoulder, pretend we've arrived in the middle of things and it's where we belong.

Take out the road map, have another look.

The lift in the air when a truck breezes past.

The highways have bloomed and bloomed until their splendour wears us out.

Flatrock, January 1, 2002

The ocean locks horns with itself,
rutting. Deeper, ponders
its own might.

Light grazes among the houses,
picks over garbage in the fence links.
Dogs bark at no one.
Freshly painted car park
on the wharf, no cars, no boats.

At night, the stars shine
like a cure that won't be discovered
for years.

Sympathy

I, I, I. Abandoned mine shafts
descending to voiceless
tunnels. Look up through the dark,
the world a pinprick above.

The blindness of perception, what we seek
never quite available, reflections skimmed
off the surface. In the garden, leaves twitch like sleeping
animals; a fly washes its face. You turn away, exhausted:
the abundance of the hidden.

At the bottom of the dark
shaft of the self, the impossible
waits behind a small window. Though you can bend
back the bars, you can't force
your way in. Denied access even to what
you most want: yourself, selfless.

Wolastoq, Spring*

As though the trees too have
predators and are ready
to flee, listening for what
they hope isn't there. Waiting
in stillness, the current barely
visible, faint tattoo
on the river's back. Floodwater.
Where swallows gather,
pale at the throats, a warning.
The clouds send down their reflections.
The difficult season.

---

* "Wolastoq, Spring" was originally titled "Saint John River, Spring" and has been changed by the author to acknowledge the river's Indigenous name. "Wolastoq" means "Beautiful River."

War in Other Countries

The sun fixes us in place. We have no option.
Plate glass windows reflect the glare
as we peer into the safety of objects, objects, objects.
The density of being here, our lives an unearned
rescue. Leisurely, wind flips back the corners
of our jackets, reveals the lining.

Distance darkens the roofs. We listen intently,
hum of electricity: fragile means to fragile ends.
Thin threads easily broken. We keep watch
over the city, unknown monument to unknown crisis.

Shelter

A suburb near the airport. You got used
to planes passing overhead, the dull roar, the pressure
in your chest as though you were underwater.
Hardly noticed the glasses rattling in the kitchen cabinet
as though they'd all had the same nightmare —
like foreign correspondents, each a report
from the fringe, trying to alert you to the possible
disaster. But you didn't believe in abroad.

When you left home you started dreaming
of planes. You sat up with your head ringing; the darkness
disoriented you, had come closer.

The enviable house in the safe hug of the cul-de-sac:
even now, you wake up from the dream
and barely hear the world around you.
Safety has stopped up your ears — it started years ago,
when the insulated walls dulled
the engines. Outside was no world
but the sprinkler-fed lawn. The glasses in the cabinet rang
like distant telephones someone else would answer.

Illusion

The light at the end of day,
shopfronts like peeling
gold, going back to the darkness
in their basements.

Bells still dangle invitingly,
but no one wants to buy.
Window displays no longer
gratify, the cash register
hardly consoling. Our urges
are like children: we will gather
them into our laps, soothe them, spend quality
time together. We've only just
realized how much they need us.

Beaten, for the moment, at the game
no one else is playing, stores slump
back to the workaday life
of goods waiting on shelves,
racks of dresses in sizes
no one wants to admit
they fit into. Cardboard boxes
in storage. They'll wait.
They've done it before.

June 15

The dandelions glow, seedlings
of light. The fields,
all arrival, laid out for something
that's just been born. Steady, steady —
first steps into afternoon.

Pretend we haven't been here
before. Pretend we don't know:
the cows gone to seed,
dandelions past their prime, shadows
in the stomach of the barn.
The emptiness of the here and now,
the end invisible, cloaked
in presence. No one asks for mercy
because where we are seems final.

Inevitable pressure of the sun. The cows
on their knees. White gloss of seeds
absorbing indecision:
                    near, nearer, nearest.

Extinction

One by one they step
onto a barge that floats on a dark
river. Boarding in no particular order, unhurried.

They don't recognize themselves in
National Geographic pictures anymore.
Something in the eyes — a lock
on a door they can't remember having
opened. They lead a parenthetical existence
inside the world they're leaving, their past lives
a small cage in which they pace.

The boat slows down in the Amazon.
It's getting crowded. They try to relax, learn
the vernacular of eternity. But even as it
carries them over the edge

of the known world: danger
in the air, the scent of what's left on Earth.
This is just the beginning.

If they could send a last message tied to the foot
of the last passenger pigeon. But it's chained
to the afterlife, gets only as far as the long-dead kings and queens
who still look greedily at the world through the wrong
end of a telescope, its beauties
tiny, receding in the convex lens.

Yet they've been disrobed; it doesn't matter now
what they decree. In eternity, they can confuse
the future with the past, make
as many mistakes as they like. They wave to CEOs

in marble-floored boardrooms. Consequences
an anchor left behind in another world.

English Daisies

When late noon
flexes its forearm,
they ripple.

So numerous; their small advice is to admit
nothing:
        not me, not me, not me...

Precipitate
of ambition, its thoughtless
plurality:

they don't ask who you are, but how many. A selfishness all
their own, a circleless inner circle
no one breaches.

Shadow slopes over
the lawn, the slow burial
at the end of day,

the daisies the last
to go.

Atget: *The Milkman's Horse*

Seized and shaken by an invisible
hand, her head a frenzy, swarm of light.
As though her very being
were a bridle she tries to shake off.

Isolated on the page as though in quarantine,
she is institutionalized behind the walls of the imaginable.
We want to touch her the way we want to touch the edge of a deep
wound. To feel light slippery on our wrists. The brightest mirror
in which everything we dread might happen.

The long exposure.
A row of dark windows behind her.
A street that could be our own.

Second View of Bell Island, October 2001

A thinking stillness.

Patience, its small, useless
vessels. The ferry boat
rocked by the ocean's
deep pendulum.

Perplexed by silence,
war opens its parachute, slips
into the ocean,
settles.

We travel quietly, so as not
to draw attention to ourselves. The waves
slip like thread
in and out of the eye of a needle.

First Snow

The pain of visibility, the trees
unbribable, backs against the sky.
No exchange. Not a way of dreaming but a persistent
wakefulness, pinching the nerves
when the heart wants to feel nothing.
Snow can be a man who still thinks of himself as a child,
invisible. But nothing is more obvious than his hunched shoulders.

Birds sink into their plumage,
shake the cold from their backs. There is too much light
and it's too strong: all you want to do is remember,
but the day insists on a witness. What's past is less than this.
Its opposite, a drift of white, settles over the lawn.

Night Fare

Taxis float like water lilies
on the slick tarmac. It's raining
too hard to walk, and it's late, they argue.
They want to take you home.

The rise and fall of your heartbeat,
cabs pulling in and out from the curb, hoping
you'll climb in. But they know too much about you,
the shine of each door a warning.
You won't give them the satisfaction.

As you walk home, the stages of sleep
uncurl like a fist in upper storeys of houses.
The night shuffles its deck of cards, plays games
with your subconscious:
                                            after you've undressed,
when you're looking out your window,
you'll see your mind galloping by. Later,
you close your eyes: the flash of mane as it turns
the corner, just before
you start to dream.

Forever

Too young to be convinced, you can't imagine
that time might turn itself inside out, showing
that what you thought was the infinite
was only its lining. Slippery and easily frayed,
your whole life a kind of magic trick.

You rehearse your own funeral, who will attend,
who will be sorry, how death will somehow prove you right.
Submerged in thoughts of this death like a bath,
right up to the neck, still breathing.

What you don't want to imagine is how far it will take you
from the known: your friends and relatives will watch your life
close into a fist, from which, when you take your last breath,
they will pull a square of bright silk. They'll slide it through their
    fingers
then let it go, watch it drift away. And when they're ready,
they'll open the fist to show it's empty.

Third View of Bell Island, December 2001

The sky's density sunken
into the soil. The invisible
come home to roost. Fields lay back
their ears, expecting a wind
that hasn't arrived.

Civilization has rubbed itself raw
on the cliffs and resents its wounds.
The ocean: train upon train arrives,
unmet, on the shore.

Nocturne

Night sky a clear-cut, stumped
with tiny stars. Sage, furred, soft and silver
in the garden. The house grows large
with silence. Sleepless. Behind every door,
a ruined city.

Time is urban sprawl: the hours go on forever.
You wait out your thoughts. Patience, virtue of solitude.

False dawn. When you sleep at last,
you become an abandoned house on a hill.
Outside, the mountains, like huge gravestones,
lie low under the stars.

THE DRUNKEN LOVELY BIRD
(2004)

Lilacs

For those who have lived
where lilacs bloom, who have lost
their immunity
              to idleness and wander through
doorway after doorway
when the lilac trees open their infinite
mauve rooms. For those
who give in and glide a little behind
their lives, a hand trailing
in the water
behind a rowboat.

Regret turns itself inside out,
like a glove
you've picked up after someone's
gone. Even the bees feel it,
sadly, sadly,
nose in the flowers,

a curtain pulled away
and there's no hand on your shoulder
to catch you before you lean too far
out the window.

A slow leak, something escaping
as soon as the petals open.
What's left grows twice
as heavy, pales,
sinks inside itself and stays
with you, a dream of which
there is not even enough left
to describe:

it is about to rain.
It is always about to rain.
These limp flowers.

Streetlight, Afternoon

It arches its long neck,
dips its head
	under the sun
like a waterbird
		bathing.
Stranded
under a blue sky,
		it watches
bicycles and skateboards, kids
in the playground...

it waits all day, has withdrawn
into the beauty of things
at rest,
	the quotidian;
preening, it blends
into the matter of fact,
almost invisible
like the noonday moon; time
to dream,
	to think of things
not otherwise noticed.

If it stretched its neck
lower, you could stroke
its metal back,
	the sun glinting
on its bent head;
though its mind is miles
away,

   it would still lean out
its throat to be smoothed.

The dull light
in its casing, the absent-minded
glow
   draws you in,
is recognizable;
it says
the distance between things
may be less
than you thought.

City Hall, August

The trees, glutted
with leaves, have ceased to grow.
Clock hands move around the dial like dogs
on the ends of leashes, bored. Time isn't worth
chasing. Children arrive on a bus
for a tour, clutch their sandwiches, go.

But this morning, soap bubbles
around the fountainhead, a foaming sculpture,
a practical joke, only let's not dwell on
who did what because here we are,
the latest group of school children running
Ne touche pas! Qu'est-ce que tu fais là? Laisse ça!
But they're beyond reproach, and they know it.

The cement angel who holds the fish that spouts
the water sits in the midst of it all, soap billowing.
Yes, clutching his green fish to his chest,
he is confessing. As if this were all his doing, or as though
he has at least done nothing to prevent it. Owning up to a measure
of humanness perhaps, a moment of weakness.
He holds his precious fish as if it were the whole world,
a trickle of water still dribbling from its mouth.
One of the teachers strides forward, and the children scatter
like pigeons. We catch sight of ourselves in their faces:
pennies just visible in the pool.

Jellyfish

Stranded, they shrink slowly into the sand,
and you have the uncomfortable feeling
of knowing more than you should,
like watching a man pretend
he isn't fat, isn't lonely, can't cry.

Mortality works itself out on the beach.
Vulnerable, it lets you touch the soft jelly of its least
protected parts. How every kind of beauty collapses
and begins again. Time waits at the centre,
almost transparent, its illegible abstractions barely
visible in the lucid, wet span of the shore. Read them
before they disappear. Bodies vanishing like the body
of this light, which dissolves without telling us why.

Cottonwood

Split husks: seed hangs
like birds just
emerged. They glisten, wait
for their wings to dry,

though others have already started
to moult, it seems, clumps
of feathers dropping
as though life took less

than a day, and so much
to remember even then. Never
has the world been more
perishable: you pass

a wedding party posing for pictures
and think of the cottonwood,
a swatch of white glimpsed
through the crowded guests.

Wanting to hold on, wanting to let go.
Break open the husk, its insides
soft and fibrous, undecided,
the seeds taken by the wind before
we've had a chance to know
how gently they resist. The pods
still hanging in the branches
turn slightly as you watch the bridal party
gather up their coats, drift away.

Refrigerator

Its life is longer
than you ever guessed;
it has travelled further
from what it knows. At night
it looks through the window
to its distant
relatives, the stars. They hum
to one another. Discuss
concepts of time
we don't understand.

When you come home
in the afternoon, it listens
to your troubles, the celibate
friend to whom you confide
everything, steadfast, the eternal
roommate whose sexless,
guileless life is a comfort.

You never know how it longs
for intelligent conversation,
can't wait for you
to sleep so it can think
of something besides the lemon
hardening at the bottom
of the crisper.

Patient, with a certain grace:
a swimmer waiting for the plunge.
Solid, rectangular, it faces
the world without regrets.
It keeps to itself, won't sleep

on the end of your bed,
but it watches. Reliable,
dependable. The habits
of an introvert: it knows when
to turn itself on and off.

Bathtub

This is all it has. It hopes it will do.

Orphaned long before you were born.

Some think it's dumb — constantly struck by surprise, that *O*.

Acoustic.

Yes, the shape of the voice inside you, talking to yourself.

An animal that has turned three circles and settled, its white edges gleaming.

The long curve of its back, the steady drip of the tap.

You splash your feet onto the tile floor.

When you go, it laps up the spilled light like a cat.

Waits for you.

Moratorium

His mind is a box of letters
folded each inside the other. He undoes them
one at a time, hopes he will never have
to open the last.

Still up before dawn. The dull glow
of the TV swamps the living room.
Old stories of codfish so plentiful you could
scoop them up. Hurts to remember
how good it was. The thought of the ocean
is an old nail hammered into his body,
rusted into him. He can't move.
At the bottom of the garden,
the boat lies naked.

He used to look down invisible stairs
into that watery basement where everything was kept,
even the gothic arch of the sky, turned over
as though in storage. The sky shames him now.
He buries himself in his armchair. His life is a small boat
in which he is afraid to stand.

Before You Were Born

They have taken a step away
from the familiar. Their lives so far
peel like paint, behind it their real existence.
Your father, at the bar,
buys your mother a drink. You are hidden,
painted into the picture but camouflaged.
No one has seen you yet.

They watch the bartender
pull the tap. It shines
like the places they hope to visit,
the plans they don't have yet.

She is a room in a house that lets the light
in slowly. His inner life rests on his face
like a lamp
he's forgotten to turn off.

The visible makes love
to the invisible. People gather
around tables, quivering,
wanting to be taken from darkness
into the flame.

In Season

The fishermen, patient and unforgiving, lines bending and glinting overhead.

Shallow water, the salmon push the door of the current open. They can't see what's ahead.

The day turning slowly into a fossil.

The fishermen try to retrieve something they've seen in the flash of mirrored bodies, fins scarring the light.

They shift their weight from leg to leg, pretend they have all the time in the world.

The cars are parked quietly under the cliff. A few leaves cling to the wet metal.

Everything is awake, listening. The trees wait like dogs.

No One Asks Leda to Dance

She stands on an island
in the goldfish pond, the tube poking
from her side as if she were a patient
escaped from hospital. If she just stands
still enough, no one will find her.

The jug she used to hold
is being cleaned or repaired;
we had no idea the water really poured
from her hip. But we were wrong
about her in all kinds of ways, a case
of mistaken identity. She is, after all,
only Leda's twin, and her destiny
is to be bronze, to continue to evade
the swan crouched at her feet,
who is no Zeus and for whom she feels sorry.

Without the jug in her upturned hands,
she seems to be asking a question, curious
not about the swan but about the weather.
She's waiting for a change, waiting
for a season less empty. She wonders
when a leaf will fall. Soon someone will come
and lead her back where she belongs.

But what happens next is what always
happens next: nothing. The swan doesn't
fan his wings, doesn't show himself
to her, doesn't unwind his looped neck.
Time has been forgotten: the thicket
of seconds doesn't rustle behind
or ahead of her; she doesn't listen for it.

There is no about-to, no rush,
no end. The fish go on spinning invisible
webs in the pool.

Goldfish

As though just born,
   fins like the thin
membranes
that swaddled them.

They hang in the water
dreaming of imperial pools
they once graced,
      swishing their tails,
waiting to return to court,

and though they might want it
as badly as anyone,
we don't remember, they say,
pretend to be caught
by surprise
      though nothing
astounds them anymore:

throw in a penny and they will change
their minds again.

Solanaceae *Datura*

1

White flowers fallen
like lost gloves,

losing shape, shrinking
when the hands are peeled
away.

No one picks them up.

2

Wheelbarrow full
of fresh, green clippings.
The branches look
down. The air, sedimented
with thought.

3

Panels of glass
let the light slip in
for a rendezvous.

If only you could lay
your hand everywhere.

4

The gardener talks about
his children. He wishes he knew
what they wanted. Carries the hose
like the feeling of failure,
an umbilical cord tying him
to every expectation he had.

5

Flowers still
hang in the branches
like white bats, wings folded.
Ribs along the length of the petals:
small, boned corsets.

6

Piped music
and a faint rumbling of planes.
Like when you lie in bed,
late in the morning, listening.
A truck grinding its gears. Your thoughts
like light pouring through glass.

7

The flowers, even those on the ground,
flare at the opening, daring. Look up
from below: a green shadow
inside, early evening.

8

The city has smeared its fingerprints
on the glass. Even the dome is grimy.
But the trees persuade you
that what you see is only
what they've imagined: there's nothing here
that doesn't belong to them. Every flower.

9

The feeling
that someone has just laid
a hand on your sleeve.
If memory
could grow a tree,
it would be this one.
The dark ground, fertilized.
The flowers.

9

The flowers.
The dark ground, fertilized.
If memory
could grow a tree,
it would be this one. The feeling
that someone has just laid
a hand on your sleeve.

8

Every flower. There's nothing here
that doesn't belong to them. But the trees
persuade you that what you see
is only what they've imagined.
Even the dome is grimy. The city has smeared
its fingerprints on the glass.

7

A green shadow inside,
early evening. Look up
from below: the flowers,
even those on the ground, flare
at the opening, daring.

6

Your thoughts like light pouring
through glass. A truck grinding its gears.
Like when you lie in bed,
late in the morning, listening.
The piped music and a faint rumbling of planes.

5

Ribs along the length of the petals:
small, boned corsets.
Flowers still hang
in the branches like white
bats, wings folded.

4

He wishes he knew
what they wanted. Carries the hose
like the feeling of failure,
an umbilical cord tying him
to every expectation he had.
The gardener talks about
his children.

3

If only you could lay
your hand everywhere.

Panels of glass
let the light slip in
for a rendezvous.

2

The air, sedimented
with thought. The branches
look down. Wheelbarrow full
of fresh, green clippings.

1

No one picks them up.

Losing shape,
shrinking when the hands are peeled
away:
    white flowers
fallen like lost gloves.

Photograph of My Mother as a Child *or* Invitation to the Wedding

You wouldn't have told it this way,
but this is the story: your aunt wearing her furs,
everyone else in double-breasted
wool coats. A ribbon perches in your hair,
but you won't smile, look into the lens as though
studying a strange animal. Your sister,
standing beside you, isn't even facing the camera,
has forgotten what she's supposed to do.
That's why you're holding her hand:
as the oldest, you remember everything,
and she is the sweet forgetful one
you long to be again.

It looks like it's snowing, soft flakes
in the thin air around you. Or it could be confetti.
Really the picture's just fading after so many years,
white flecks in the paper. And yours is the only
tiny face that knows what's happened.
If everyone else came to life, like a movie, like a dream,
they would look around in amazement, exclaiming,
"Where are we?" "How pretty the snow is!"
"Don't you look smart!" "The church seems so small!"
Like children, revolving, faces radiant
with lack of understanding, not yet realizing
they can't brush the white flakes
from their coats.

You don't move, look time in the eye
as you would a growling dog
on the way to school. They'll discover the truth
soon enough, and if not, so much the better.
That it snows in places you've never seen

and that time can't be harnessed
is not something everyone can understand.
And it *is* like the first snow as they laugh and smile,
though you will only go so far.
They thought this photograph
would tell them something. Still looking
into the camera, you wonder why
you should stop pretending now.

Barbershop

The hollow, earthly light
at the end of day. He's going
home soon, but no need to rush.
He snips more quickly only
to show his deftness: to keep the hands
moving, it is the old way, he says.

The old ways make us nervous;
we've seen ghosts lingering in the shop.
The blades rub against one another, a habit,
like a drink after a hard day.

He finishes, glances into the mirror
as if into our thoughts. A shiver
as though the room were a field of grass.
He holds up a hand mirror so you can see the back.
The light outside has changed as the shape
of your face changed, the suddenly
tender scalp exposed under the shorn hair.
You nod, pay up.

                Light pours in
like the accumulation of the day's labour.
We take a look backward as we go,
as if we've forgotten something,
some token we need to get into the next day.

Too late, he's already sweeping up.
As we rejoin the crowded street, a superstition
lingers in my mind:
your hair in a ring around you on the floor.

The Drunken Lovely Bird

was the signature on a letter in a dream. The man who wrote it had a high forehead and slim hands.

Shelley: a mind like a church.

Skylarks.

He might have been the one in the dream — I say this because when I woke up I thought it seemed a good name for a boat, something to sail away in, something from which to throw off ropes on a summer's day.

So I think of Shelley in Italy, floating down the canals.

Of Shelley, at sea, drowning.

Of the blithe Spirit.

The bird that never was, come to rescue us into springtime, give us a measure of loveliness to hold on to and to let go.

Of: not to possess but to imagine.

You see, this was the dream of springtime, also of leaving. I remember short skirts and tennis courts, sunlight like large sliding doors, oaths and promises.

Italy shorthand for loss. Tennis also. The courts where we play, the children he wanted to keep, love. Things you want to be and go on being.

1820: a passion for sailing.

Teach me half the gladness.

Of: where every poem begins and lets go, even in dreams,
the drunken lovely bird.

Orpheus Meets Eurydice in the Underworld

Still limping, she has come. She waits at the foot of the hill, doesn't dare go further, remembers how it once vanished under her feet.

She has spent the time thinking about her wedding day, tracing the mark on her ankle where the serpent bit. It hasn't healed yet; perhaps it won't until he comes back. She has never desired his death, but wished for it as one wishes for rain.

The steep hill, where it led and couldn't lead. So many times.

When he arrives he looks more tired than she can understand. The lyre has vanished; they stand together silently.

Even as she remembers his face, she loses something else. She has been alone so long now; how often she has stood here, how much she has wanted to climb.

She takes him home, puts him to bed then slips in beside him. His childhood bed, too short for him now; they will have to find another.

They waken slowly. As ghosts they pass through each other's bodies; she puts her hand into his heart. He had been worried she would forget.

They play in the fields, run races, drift through tall grasses carelessly, as only those who have had to wait forever can. They have a private sign language; no one speaks in this place; even the streams are still.

Sometimes when they are walking she teases him, falls behind. He looks over his shoulder again and again: there she is. They never tire of this game.

Home from Danceland

The headlights, the mute engine like the feeling
of what it was to be, long ago,
in someone's arms. Vibrations
as though it were sifting through
our pasts. The car windows
reflective, lost in thought. The daisies
drooping in your hair. We had found our way
under the peeling rainbow painted over
the door of Danceland. Waltzes and polkas
still play in our ears, faintly,
a miniature Danceland revolving in our heads.

History wants to repeat itself, a song
it can't stop humming. Just one more time,
one last dance. We felt it when we walked in.
Nostalgic, the rolls of horsehair under the floor
wanted to be nursed, gently
reminded of the rhythms
that ran over them in the twenties,
the thirties, the hand that caressed
a hip, a shoulder. They wanted
to hear the tapping
of feet like rain on the roof when
everything you love is safe
or already lost, and there's nothing
to do but remember. Like being eighty,
your brother dead in the war, husband dead,
your sister waltzing with you because
who else is there? Like being six
and sleeping wrapped
in your father's coat, waiting until they're tired

and your mother slips off her shoes,
time to go home.

The way memory persists, and we
cater to it. We stare through our reflections
as we drive home, looking past
ourselves as though we were already ghosts.
The darkened fields. Danceland spins
in the mind like a decorated cake,
a music box. Those of us who love
to dance and those who came
to please, to watch: everyone took a turn
on the floor, spinning on the rims
of imagined decades. A glance.
A flicker of something like recognition
and then it's gone.

BREAKER
(2008)

Surrender

Sometimes the light, a horse,
gallops into the room
and demands you surrender.
It paws the floor, snorts —
and so you rise out of the low-lying
cloud of the self, the half-dreaming
wakefulness we call love,
and into the cool air of the real.

It shakes its mane impatiently,
rears and kicks, its beautiful body
insisting on what it wants,
pushing its way in. Not
that you're afraid, not exactly.
But it shines straight into your eyes.
And though the heart is small
and cramped, barely large enough for
your own wants, you retreat into a corner,
make do with less. Your only choice
when the world lifts its head
and clarity pours from its back.
Filling the room.

Wonder

Your mind has emerged
from the night's cold furnace
bright and shining, the dross
washed away. A blue sky has risen
in place of the welter of stars.

As sleep's paralysis slowly fades,
the soul looks around, hoping
for a glimpse of its origin. Tick tock.

The new day hangs from the teeth of yesterday,
which still roams like a lion, prowling through
furniture enshrined in shadow. You have woken up
inside the world's subconscious glittering mind,
have caught it dreaming as it will go on dreaming all day
under the surface of what you know — a banked fire,
invisible, odourless.

We Hope It Will Be Quick

We hope it will be quick, painless,
will happen in our sleep. And that if our minds
give way, there will remain an "I" whose collapse
completes an arc, effortlessly.

So many short straws, and so much conspiring
to lengthen the ones drawn. We hope for strength,
something to help us go on then to give up
even that crutch. However sputtering,
leaky, convulsive, we want to dwell in the world
without condition, even as it ends. We practise
deep in our bodies a fierce acceptance that may be impossible
to achieve, especially now that summer has come,
the day silting into us, heavy fragrance of clover
manuring the lungs.

Sometimes the world seems better for its shortcomings,
what it can't become. The clover expands
like an ocean across the field, sends itself out and out,
never coming back.

Pawel Laughing on the Beach
after a photograph by Nan Goldin

Pawel has just come out of the freezing winter sea, has put on his pants and stands, chest bare, in a warm reddish light. His arms are crossed protectively over his chest, but his head's thrown back, laughing — the devil in him tempting fate.

Oh, his radiant skin, the ripple of bones, his chest and arms, his sweet neck! Oh, the soft hairs clustered at his navel. He's doing a favour for his friend Nan, who's always taking these pictures, and because of her and because of the salt and the sun, he's feeling so good he doesn't care that the world will eventually pound him to dust and that it's battering him even now. The sun's delicious and he doesn't give a damn about anything else — so birth and death shrug their shoulders and relinquish their hold on him.

This life and the one afterward want each other, they do. We can feel them trembling (as Pawel is trembling after the cold, cold sea), feel the tug as they strain to come together and are forced apart. It's impossible, except in instants like this, Pawel's arms crossed in memory of suffering while he laughs in delight, his body turned daringly to the camera, dead on — for he has opened his heart to the blood of its next existence even as it pumps in his chest. Somehow, he has stepped into another life, straddles them both. And he's aglee, getting away with this for even a split second. After all, he didn't seek it out, can't be blamed for this glitch in the mechanics. And the lens will be refocused in the next second anyway, as it must be, for if it went on — well, it can't go on, it just can't.

Days without End

Spring rages
like a fire in the house,
wants to eat
every splinter.

It forces its way
into buds that explode
like pockets of gas.
Tears new life from the thin
tissue of what was.
The ground shivers.
The trees ache
under the pressure,
look to the sky
for a cool blue rain,

a sign that God
doesn't sit idly by
while creation burns,

that He, too, endures
the heat of His love,
the great fire
He's pushed upon
the living.

Vanity

So beautiful it can afford to be careless,
the tree has dropped handfuls of white petals
and now leans down to admire itself
in the fragrant pool.

Take even a single flower, see how it mirrors
itself and how pleasing you find
the symmetry. Like you, it wants the world
to be endless — headless and tailless. It wants to be repeated,
again and *again*, for despite its lustre and ghostly appeal,
despite the way its radiance is dispersed across
the field of light, it, too, is a stranger.
So badly does it want to regain the intimacy
before it knew to cry *again* that it tries
to drown out the rest of the world,
multiplying itself in the eye until nothing else
can enter. And you don't try to stop it.
If anything, you open your eyes wider,
for the impact is gentle compared
to the loneliness that grips you when you
look around and see the green, filtered light,
the matter-of-fact gravel, the slow but steady
differentiation of leaves,

thoughtful and private. Each thing so separate,
so painfully distant, that you begin to pin your hopes
on the impossible, praying that the flower-image
will find a way through, will destroy the masonry
and emerge from the cloud of plaster into another realm.
And you might follow, give up the apparatus of the mind
and step into a place where telling the difference between
this and that means nothing. You'd give almost anything

if you could find a place like that, if anyone could,
if such a place could be said to exist. A place
where the tree and all its flowers are indistinguishable
from the Earth itself. Where time falters. Where the eye
blinks and is done.

Dead Pelican, Point Lobos
after Edward Weston's photograph of the same name, 1942

The slumped neck, slack-skinned gullet,
the prehistoric, leathery eyelid
fallen forward like a person leaning over
a table, exhausted. A wing half unfolded,
the head limp as though a string has snapped.

You half expect it to stir now that you're here,
but the body is already withdrawing from its old habits,
wet feathers plastered to the throat.
It shames you, who want to own the creaturely
beauty but not the death, not the body
oozed like oil onto the beach.

You feel overhead the sky's abandoned
consciousness, the blue of its withdrawn eye.
There should be peace in this.
For when the will is gone, what's left
but grace, the mere force of being?
The sand grinds underfoot as you turn to go,
fearing the separation of body and soul
but unable to explain, even to yourself,
why it should be so.

Fish

His body flings itself into the air
then slaps back down,
a great guffaw. The walloping
seems to have exhausted the whole pond,
which retreats into a deeper solitude.
Insects hum nervously.

It's midsummer, and there is no rest.
The fish concentrates, the willows concentrate,
the old abandoned tire concentrates. It's a risk:
the balance tips as the sun's great incinerator
burns up past lives, claims all our possibilities.
And because some part of us wants to follow it,
the other part resists: the sap rises, blood surges,
keeps us hard at it, pushing our way out
as though the struggle to be born had not ended.

There's an urgency in the slow-paced afternoon:
the fish jumps and snaps at flies not just because
he's hungry but because he's a fish, and this
is his attempt to assert himself. He feels the force
of heaven, the blurred horizon looming in the distance.
He feels the danger. And in the murky water
he's pooling, readying to jump again.

Big East Lake

This is the world, impenetrable, the flat
black pupil that doesn't look at you.
You want to be wooed, to praise it;
instead, you're bored: beauty, what of it?

You feel yourself at the bottom of a well;
love of the landscape can't be roused.
Nature has shifted into your blind spot,
no longer a vision, no longer your ego
revealed to itself. The trees immersed
in growth, occupied by their own being.
The water slips off your paddle.
The shore slips into the water's darkness.

You shift uncomfortably in the bow,
haven't the heart for this.
The light travels a little slower here.
The trees quieter, sober.
If it weren't too late, you'd go back
on whatever promise brought you here.

Breaker

A cold-burning brilliance,
distillery of light, green camouflaged
in the ocean's understorey. Your mind is gathered
like a horse about to take a hurdle, ready to leap.
But fascinated by the rising wall, it stalls,
and time seems to slow
while you consider the monumental
fatigue of this imminent failure.

Beauty like a stain bleeds through
the layers of matter,
                       something, somewhere in pain,
the traces of it seeping into this world.
You stand back and watch as the inevitable
takes over: the green recess
of the wave collapses, the light buckles,
the depths recover what was owed.
How helpless you are, yet
on the brink of being able to do more,
as though you could punch your hand through
the window to rescue whatever it is that,
trapped inside, haunts the corridors.
You haven't, though, quite got what it takes.
The window shatters anyway, but in the spirit
of denial. So it goes, the heartbreak
of merely standing by as what
dwells here does its living and dying
on its own terms.

Away

The voices first, echoing
and tinny, as though trapped inside
an old radio. Then two men with tool kits,
*X*s of reflective grey tape across their backs.
They walk side by side along the rails,
toward whatever strangeness inhabits the tunnel,
their muffled footsteps giving nothing away.
They are fading out of time as we know it,
walking into the dimness of an ever-delayed present.
From where I stand, looking into darkness,
the tunnel is not just a tunnel, the *X*s not just *X*s.
They shimmer meaningfully.

Big, well-fed men a few years beyond middle age,
backs evoking old-fashioned bravado,
talking about home with a shrug of the shoulders.
They amble along the tracks, swinging
their flashlights, light zipping across the dank walls.
The zigzagging light is panicked, groping
for the tunnel's low arc. It's the animal in us
seeking the dimensions that comfort
blind consciousness. Something to hold onto.

They're getting smaller, the *X*s smaller,
and my fear for them also recedes,
turns into loneliness. I want to call out,
warn them about some fate they seem already
to know and have accepted. No reason to speak of it,
say their backs. And it's ridiculous, but I could cry,
have in fact to prevent myself. Watching them
go as though they're already gone, passengers
washing through the station, the crowd pressing

around me. And suddenly I seem to see everything, everything!
A delusion, of course: just as quickly it all goes black.
The flashlight beams the last thing I see.

Into the Open

The heavy, stagnant night gives way —
frogs stop grunting as the overheated
sky releases a spasm of light.

The surface of the lake
loses dimension, falsely vivid.
We flatten against the walls
of ourselves as though at knifepoint,
the body spotlit, exposed,
faults glaring.
For an instant everything on Earth
loses consciousness, goes limp.
In the ruptured darkness
we grasp what we can and look within.
We prepare to resist the divine spark
that attracts the lightning,
draws it down.

As quickly as it traps us, we are released,
but whatever it is out there that wants us
has taken shape,
and we're still stricken when darkness returns.
We've seen the world waver,
know it could hand us over, hostages
to blind force. If there's a name for what happened,
we've already forgotten it.
The sky is empty,
the lake's borrowed face:
we could see clear down to the bottom
and still not understand.

Nesting

Swans groom the light,
prune it with a clip
of their wings, drift
through the clustered lilies.
To the left, stuck
in the shallow mud, a tire:
fat bruised lip, thick
black slug curled into itself,
water lisping around it.
The swans brush against the rim,
consider it a moment
then clamber up industriously,
assuming a purpose
in the worn treads, the functional
given up to the mud's stubborn
suck. By next week
the swans have gathered reeds
and dirt, clay and sticks
into an island, the tire buried
so that everything we've made so far
seems only a beginning,
a crude variation of a kind
of manufacture that ebbs and flows,
hums to itself under its breath.
Nesting, at home, the swans preen
with the insouciance of those
who haven't had to ask forgiveness.
They are not withdrawn,
turn the eggs over in the nest.
Are not lonely.

Fourth View of Bell Island, January 2, 2003

A blue glow, the sky's
depths dredged up.

Abandoned mines,
another junkyard of human
pain, loss. Another hole
in the Earth's intestines.

The old houses, naked,
gradually reconcile themselves
to what has gone.
Perhaps there can be a slow
recovery of what we owe:

something here is still alive
enough to feel fear,
and braces itself
against its past, clings
to the old familiar pain.
What has been taken
can be taken again,
the wound not yet so deep
that it's been scraped clean.

Endurance

The city huddles in its lit cave,
glittering. Snow spins under car wheels;
the heart seizes up as cold seeps into the arteries
and your higher feelings slowly give way,
contract. Your mind begins turning
to stone as the old mineral worry creeps in,
fear of decay, the toil toward oblivion.
Too tired to protest, already feeling
the hardening of the sorrows that relieve
the distances between us, you allow it.
Even the beloved is just a face
pressed under ice.

The snow falls and falls. You endure
the slow shift through the equatorial
from love to loss. Even so, you crane
your neck toward the gauzy clouds,
the snowflakes drifting past the street lights
carelessly, as though sightseeing,
all the time in the world. They are marred
only by the imperfection of gravity,
which carries them down to vanish underfoot.
The compromise is struck. The brown slush
in the gutters pains you. The lit sky pains you.
Nothing that does not leave its mark.

View from the Train

Wheat stalks drowse away the afternoon,
steep in their unshaken, golden selves,
a tableau of contentment. The Earth's heavy,
glowing cargo steadied and sleeping
a deep sleep: the shadows have loosened,
drifted away, migrating into the forest to roost.

Inside the bright gloom of the train
a semi-conscious haze: the smudged glass
imposes a drag on light, which slows
to a standstill. You drink in the slumbering
fields, heady, thoughtless, the sway of the train
like your mind, like a dream swimming
through the narrow canals of waking thought.
Relinquishing hold, you drift into
the thick, golden liquidity of the fields,
weighted and at ease.

But even as your mind blurs, the dark line
of your vision enters the fields like a fox.
It parts the grasses, separating this from that,
blade from blade. Stealthily, it sneaks past
the sleeping guard of the mind and goes
about its business: determines which is which,
staking out the distance between the risen stalks.
It seeks to lose itself but instead parts the grasses
from their kind and thrusts them into singularity,
naked and alone. The stillness you felt earlier
was not stillness; the train moves on.
And then? Does the gap seal over
in your absence, a meniscus of light?

The air in the car is sour with the breath
of strangers. You shut your eyes, think about never
opening them again. But spots of colour drift by
even under your lids. The train pushes steadily on,
repeating the same clicks and clacks, chugging along as if
it will never stop, as if it's forgetting how,
as if it couldn't stop even if it tried.

At Grenadier Pond

1

The willow stands stock-still,
its long leaves like knives divorced
from use so they're no longer knives,
just sharp-edged and glinting.
They don't remember what they're for,
a thousand tiny incarnations
of forgetfulness,
multiple and separate.

2

In its array of not-knives, the willow
leans into itself, supporting its purposeless
cavalry. It seems to be arguing a cause
beyond cause, something inherent in the way
time opens and closes its wings
like an insect poised on a blade of grass.

3

The slow yellowing of leaves
proceeds as though it were a muscle
flexing in sleep, meaninglessly.
Not a yea or nay but a silent, emphatic *is*,
like a person who has done the same work
every day of their life, could do it, they think,
if they were dead, so that even their dreams
are a ritual of the present.

4

The trees shift, sway like pack horses,
the weight of non-being equal
to the muscular thrust of all that pushes
into the light, each opened eye. Of the mistaken
belief that life can be made to sit quietly
in the palm of the hand and not tremble,
not much is said.

Exposed

You almost tripped over them: blunt scissors
left to rust in the thick, upholstered lawn.
Heavy, they made you feel the seriousness
of the July heat. Their weight was conducted into you —
six years old and you began to feel your presence as force.
The scissors were both tool and unalloyed consequence.
You dropped them, not quite ready.

Afterward, the quietest afternoons made you nervous,
the rustle of curtains. Summer grinding away.
You turned dead flies over on the windowsill
so their stomachs wouldn't be exposed — biding your time,
waiting to see who'd move first, you or the unknown
person inside you, the untrustworthy being whose small crimes
you wouldn't commit. In the garden you'd realized
what was possible — it struck you like a match.
But you didn't want it to go on burning.

The weight of that strange July afternoon
is still welded into you, added density in the bone.
You don't expect to be freed, but sometimes, in dreams,
the burden transforms itself. The body becomes landscape
and a train flashes through, balanced on the twin rails
of the heart. It disappears into the world beyond,
vanishes in a cloud of dust, and you are empty,
are the middle of nowhere. Alone and suddenly
fearful, you look around for the familiar shadows
that give things shape; there are none. Panicky,
you squint toward the horizon: there, like a mirage,
are the scissors, hanging in the sky. They invite you
to pluck them down, hanging there as if they were destiny,
but you refuse them, have decided your life is not this.

You clasp your hands, squeeze your eyes shut,
hope to wake up before the desire
to reach for them overwhelms you.

Quiet

The sky a deadbolt slid firmly
into place. The Earth is lonely:
a dog barks its head off, trapped
in the slow afternoon. When he gives up,
the silence is another lock on the door.

The heart pushes on us like a stone
no one can lift. We want so much
from this life but can only glimpse it.
We wander from room to echoing room,
always only the surface of what we seek:
smoke rising through the floorboards, the faint
perfume of the Earth burning, deep in the well of itself.
That something we have never seen affects us so completely:
we are the healed skin of its molten core.

Tell It to the Night

I

Nobody loves you
like the one who left you—
the hard truth you're weary of,
wanting to forget, the blues
taking you into the heart of trouble
so deep you can't remember
how you got here. Dancing close,
the body giving up its shame,
swaying in the emptiness that's left
when what could have been drifts away,
your arm draped hopelessly
over someone's back like a sigh,
like the matter in the body sighing,
envious of the spirit, its longevity.

The instruments shine, feel within them
the same loneliness,
attracted by the beautiful sheen
of sweat on your skin. The notes sink
deeper into the night, into your skin,
prodding you gently, recalling you to your sadness,
for it's late now, time to remember all that has
gone wrong, all that has been lost,
all that has left you here,
music's slow liquor passing through you
as all that mattered has
passed through and gone on.

II

After a beer break, the band reappears,
faces gleaming. We're bold and uneasy.
The melody begins, a run of notes —
the trumpet shines. The floor
quivers under our feet like a horse,
all muscle, ready to run.

As the bass player picks up the pace,
the old hall quakes. We dance past midnight
under the aegis of the past. Our weight
pushes nails out of the boards;
between sets, a man in a blue suit
taps them back in, careful
as though this were the spine of the living.

Evening

Swallows skim the pond, lilting,
tweak insects from the air.
They cross and recross an invisible border,
bodies gleaming with purpose,
violet backs armoured against doubt.
You imagine them tucked under a cliff, sleeping
when the winds blow in from the cold eternal.

With evening, your mind feels a loss
of habitat, disorienting. The blurred, long-distance
sighting of immortality as sleep closes in.
The salt of dreams is deposited behind
your eyes, a glimpse of the distinctions mined
from the visible. Confirmation of your poor,
Earthbound status, for what are dreams
but the mind running over and over its lack?
God, if there is a God, doesn't dream.
You wonder if the sparrows do — they must —

for they, like you, inhabit a shadowed world.
Yet they seem to sleep unharmed while you
are up late again, worrying. In the dark unsheltered sky,
even the stars seem to have filtered out doubt:
they shine in the coal-black night, raw and enviable,
not fragments but each one the whole you've lost.

Suburbs

Night holds up a mirror on all sides;
there is a depth in things you haven't accounted for.
The bungalows return your gaze; their lost dignity
surfaces and they stare at you, trying
to import meaning into their small lives.

Vinyl-sided, slow-witted,
they insist they didn't mean for this to happen,
this sameness, shackled to their own kind
like cattle transported slowly nowhere
in a broken-down truck. This is what happened to them,
not what they are. And they know the privilege
of even this adequate existence. Ashamed,
they lower their heads as children do
who think they have done something wrong
in being born. You, too, bow your head,
wish you could divest yourself of scorn.
A woman climbs into a car, will drive until
the motor dissolves her troubles.
Further up the street a man lifts a blind,
looks around, and wonders what it can all be for.
He hopes no one will answer.
He is embarrassed to have to ask.

Waiting

Night lays its weary head
against your roof, settles in.
Roses swell in the dark.

In neighbouring houses, children stare
at televisions like theologians. The stars
no longer visible, no longer means to an end.

Comfort comes slowly
as you climb into bed and sleep loosens
the bandages. In your dreams
you hear the trees rustle and whisper and hiss
their disappointment. For you are not

the serum, not the powerful, Herculean,
mythical, myth-bearing creature they need.
If only you could whisper back,
tell them how much they mean to you.
But it wouldn't matter:
fact is, they're waiting for someone.
And you are not that someone.

Waiting for the Forks

The things that can and do
go wrong: Grandfather's birthday, a family reunion,
and no forks for the cake

because the caterers had a lot on their minds,
what with the champagne and Aunt Julie
in her thigh-high kimono —

in fact, no one realized until now, so what can we do
but make airplanes from folded napkins,
nibble the frosting and kick the dog

under the table while they fetch forks
from down the street, which will take a while,
but that's okay because Grandfather

has a lot to remember, enough candles on the cake
to light the darkest corners of his mind; suddenly he can see
all the rooms of his life, and he was planning to make

a speech, has been trying to think of just what to say,
waiting for it to come, but now surprises himself by deciding
he won't speak, won't reveal himself, not to a soul,

and when he's in heaven he won't come back
and tell them what it's like. He's just this minute
decided he'll step through the last door

willingly, and that means no backward glances.
Besides, what if he tries to come back
and can't? What if the threshold vanishes

as soon as he crosses it? And even if he could reappear,
they might not recognize him — though that's
hard to imagine. In any case, his mind is made up,

and he hopes they'll make the best of it.
A camera appears and he poses obligingly
with a pair of grandsons on his lap,

the children's hair wispy and colourless as his,
their eyes fixed on him as his are fixed
on the red crepe paper-covered table:

waiting for the forks, waiting for the camera to flash,
he looks at the plate in front of him, the slice of cake
he's about to eat.

Breakwater

In the 1990s a breakwater was built using erratics that once dotted the shore of Flatrock, Newfoundland. Erratics are blocks of rock dropped by retreating glaciers.

The boulders lifted from the shore,
raised in slings as though being rescued.
Embarrassed, their awkward bodies
dangled in mid-air as though they had been
woken from sleep, taken unprepared.
Piled like rubble in the bay,
they stare out from the breakwater
as if forbidden to speak, using ancient
telepathy to send a warning.

We were afraid of something they
represented, their blank faces
looking sombrely into the future,
monuments to a mistake we had yet
to make, traces of something
we wanted to erase before it could exist.
We haven't eluded it. No better off,
we've forfeited consolation, won't know
where to go in our grief.

We've cast ourselves deliberately out
of our own future; it is a locked door
on which we will bang and bang,
looking for answers, looking for silence,
a moment to think through our lives
before they're lost.

Falling from a Great Height

A hardened, varnished afternoon.
Gulls pick at dumpsters
as boys ferry their basketball back and forth
over the centreline, stewards of the court.
Heat pours off the tarmac; they play deeply,
soulfully, until the day lopes off to the western
horizon and the game loses its appeal.

They go inside as darkness trembles
over the neighbourhood like an alcoholic's hand.
A car passes; the sound of its engine wraps our minds
in its cocoon. We close our eyes, forget at last
what we're made of and sink into the elsewhere
that cast its invisible shadow all day.
Heat drifts from room to room
not wanting to disturb anyone.

The garbage rots leisurely in the dumpster,
its rich odour attracting raccoons. Inside,
children and adults dream of changing places,
long for each other in the dark.

Sixth View of Bell Island

The ferries pass like strangers.
All night Heaven and Earth
draw closer together,
threatening to collapse
into each other.

Old unforgiving loves hold us
accountable. Their claims ferment
in the blood as we stand here,
waiting for a pathway to open
in our brains, hoping
something will click.

The ferries have memorized
themselves, no longer need the mirror
each offers. They file past
with no sign of recognition.
We feel an irreducible shiver:

failure begins to seem a refuge.
As though once admitted,
it will demand nothing more of us.

Waves place their hands carefully
on the shore, wait for the moon
to tug them away.

Longing

Tired of being alone, especially at night.
The stars broken down in the sky, engines stalled,
shining, waiting for rescue.
The height of things stares down at you.

You settle into the night's own loneliness,
let the universe expand, stretch like a curing hide.
Someday the absence on the other side
will show through, unquantified:
if history is an animal, this is its pain,
an unspoken reproach, the throbbing in the vein
that accompanies the inevitable going forth,
you or someone like you taking the place
of the unborn, feeling their stare.

Is the great beauty of things somehow visible to itself?
If so, is it enough? For how quickly it vanishes,
becomes its own ghost. And then there is you:
you have only the barest idea of what you'll leave behind.
History must feel its failures vividly.
You wonder if it heard the chorus fade away
when you were born, for you grew up
knowing nothing of the echoes that surrounded you,
still less of the voices that will be lost when you leave.

Asleep

A wasp-like hum in the room,
the something-going-on that passes for silence
in these quarters, for we want to believe in silence,
that our repose leaves nothing behind, empties all the chambers,
takes the present into our dreams with us and leaves
a void that works like acid on all that was.
Car headlights on the wall mean nothing,
the cramped, ungrowing furniture, nothing,
the church spires, tired bells, nothing.
They are but the residue of day, less than echoes,
the last creaking stair on the way out of perception.
We have come to an agreement: tired of the world
in its inalienable unlikeness, we will give up coaxing it out.
So the night darkens, the curtain drifts
out the window, the very lateness of the hour ceases.
We sleep side by side with eternity, and never touch.

HEAVEN'S THIEVES
(2016)

Winter in the Garden

Everything sleeps.
The serpent curls around the roots of the apple tree,
which is bare. The leaves have not gone, but have changed
into thought. Last year's apples lie under a bed of snow.
In spring they'll rise into the branches again.
Meanwhile they dream, sometimes of the legendary
chunk of apple carried down to Earth in Eve's stomach,
though the real meaning of *fallen* eludes them:
in jobless towns along the US–Mexico border
80% of the young men want to be hired assassins.
What can Eden find to compare to this?
Wanting to lead *some* kind of life
while it's still possible. Maybe the blaze of sun across the snow,
maybe that. But not the drip, drip, drip of the melt
as paradise wakens. Not the bright sky.
Nothing that has not had to die.

Heaven's Thieves
after the still lifes of Pieter Claesz, ca. 1597-1660

The fish, a drizzled oily silver,
dozes beside crusts of white bread. A cluster of grapes overflows
its goblet, each blowing its own pale bubble, bored
like every other painted thing, as though the game
has been played,

as though I could pluck the knife from the carved frame
and the fish, the fruit, would go on floating in their paint slick, too
    well-fed
to have an eye for consequence yet strangely
dissatisfied — fatty, iridescent, clinging to half-lives even as they divide
and diminish to a nothing that radiates like the thought of gold
in the minds of its inheritors.

The light is Promethean:
let it pour over you, let it shine in the eyes
of whoever looks your way, let even the damage gleam and be satisfied,
which is what the fish and wine and fruit are doing, look:
simmering in the stubborn sun, paraded on the table like subdued
    peacocks,
plates dressed in the spoils
of a ransacked heaven. Betrayal is in the air. But impossible to steal

from rich for poor without a little of this, and there are beauties
willing to do the job.
I mean the beauty that's willing to sleep its way out of a tough
    situation,
willing to not-quite-die for its cause. Even the grapes,
even the half-peeled lemon: lying there brazenly,
clothed in stolen bounty, flaunting their ill-begotten skins.

Ends of the Earth[*]
one millihelen = the amount of beauty sufficient to launch exactly one ship
  — Bureau internationale des poids et mesures

How many ships are launching today,
in this late September sun? How quickly

do they run aground, and are they more
beautiful as ruin, spilling gold

over the road, which floods and thus
lifts them up again, resurrected?

That may have been what Ashbery meant
by *the double dream of spring*, only this

is autumn, almost, mostly,
and that way of talking — *autumn, spring* —

may be too simple for what's going on.
We launch ships upon ships,

failed attempts to reach the ends
of the Earth, the final *amen*, the dream

doubled and redoubled in an even-now-
I-hope, quixotic ship of fools setting out

full sail, here in the complications,
under the late millihelenial sun.

---

[*] The attribution of the definition of the millihelen to the BIPM was made in a footnote to a philosophy paper of which the author no longer has a record. Editorial research suggests that the millihelen and its definition may be a joke from a 1954 edition of *Punch* magazine.

Loving Pavlova

Voyager 1, four billion miles from Earth, sent back a photograph. It used to hang in a NASA auditorium, seemed unremarkable, a few streaks of light on a black background, but about halfway down, toward the right, you could find the tiniest revelatory blue speck.

And almost every visitor who saw that barely-there dot touched it: the image got worn, like the steps of public buildings. It kept having to be replaced.

Why not give in to beauty, consider its truth?

Anna Pavlova danced the swan in a perfect white tutu. She had a dessert of meringue and cream named after her. She also had bad teeth — really terrible. Ruinous. There's almost no footage of her *Dying Swan*, but there are photographs, and in some she's smiling, mouth open.

Her audiences didn't care. They wanted to sit in darkened auditoriums and watch, feel the hush of the swan sinking to the floor then applaud it back to life.

To imagine things are better than they are, that is, to look to the best in them. This isn't a lie, or if a lie, only partly so —

I have a small photograph of Pavlova. Dressed in her swan costume, she poses against a black drop cloth, head tilted to one side, eyes downcast. She seems suspended there — no bigger than my thumb, but I can see every vane of her feathers, even the down pinned to her shoulders.

When, standing in the NASA centre, you finally find us — that fleck of blue — it's almost impossible not to reach out. Gently, as though you could feel the weight of your finger from miles away.

Who can help but think of things as we hope them to be — and isn't this hope the whitest of lies? A lie so pale you can barely see it.

The *Voyager* photograph asks you to imagine yourself so far from Earth, it's like rehearsing your own death. I don't mean picturing your funeral, more like trying to count the individual feathers sewn into her costume.

Pavlova died for real at age forty-nine, her breath laboured as if after a performance. She asked for her tutu, had it laid out on the bed beside her, all those dying swans,

not lies really, just the most bearable part of the truth.

Oranges for Adorno[*]

Natural beauty shares the weakness of every promise with that promise's inextinguishability.
    — Theodor Adorno

Large-pored, swaddled in pith, they swell
in the Andalusian heat. Each tree has promised itself
right up from the ground, branches full of dying suns,
fallen soldiers. Purveyors of false hope —
as though, having let go the branch, one could yet
hang from it, uneaten. But wasps chew at the rinds,
determined that no fruit will go unforaged,
so the longed-for apotheosis comes
to naught — unless we count the lives of insects
as our own, which we may do, bound together as we are.
To say it otherwise: what if Time were indeed a god?
And if all who live have their part
in its immortality, wearing its groove deeper
with their passing, each scarred and bitten communicant?
Pick the orange, scour the rind, eat and feel its sugars
spike your bloodstream: its fate both fulfilled and open-ended,
a promise carried forward in you, ever incarnate.

---

[*] The epigraph is from Theodor Adorno's *Aesthetic Theory*, trans. Robert Hullot-Kentor.

The Invention of Beauty

The swan especially doesn't
seem real anymore, so we ignore
his arched neck
                beckoning, inviting us to slip off the
noose, asking us to swoon
like we used to

as he glides undialectically along,
dipping his sovereign head
into the mirror
                and emerging again, unchanged,
unfathomed,

trailing past in invisible quotation marks
as if hundreds of versions of himself didn't float
in his wake,
              a raft of platitudes —

as if he were truly just a single
swan a-swimming on a sunny
summer's day.

1st Corps de Ballet

There was a man mistook himself for the sun,
for fire. He trained assiduously.
He danced because that's what fire does,
especially in the pit of the eye. *To command
the eye is to command the man*; he was no fool.
Ruler since the age of four, he entertained
no comparison of the arch of his foot
but to the firmament. It was discussed
alongside the tenderness of quail and other
delicate matters. Apollo was his role of choice.
His ballet master replaced him sometimes
so the King could witness his own glory.

Red Dye No. 40[*]

There is no excellent beauty that hath not some strangeness in the proportion.
   — Francis Bacon

That was the summer the bees turned red, really truly red.
Even the eyes of the comb were red,
fiery and swollen as though suddenly allergic
to their own kind.

The apiarist was appalled:

McDonald's red, the red of stoplights, cough drops,
cinnamon hearts, bodega roses. Of tandoori chicken,
scarlet letters flashing past like tail lights —

*I thought maybe it was coming
from some kind of weird tree, maybe a sumac,*
but the trail led to a syrupy mine tailing, the sloppy vats
in a maraschino cherry factory,

survivor of the American decline
in domestic goods and still supplying cherries
as it had since 1948, the yard swimming
in fluorescent runoff the bees sucked up through
reddening proboscises.

One and a half million cherries a day, sent out in jars
labelled in cursive,
a long *h* curving to the right like a stem.

---

[*] The epigraph is from Francis Bacon's essay "Of Beauty." Italicized lines within the poem are quotes from apiarists Cerise Mayo and David Selig, as found in the November 29, 2010, *New York Times* article "The Mystery of the Red Bees of Red Hook," by Susan Dominus.

I started reading about dyes,
found a website that sells a dye to detect cancer cells:
1 mg in your shopping cart for $242 US.
It bonds with the tumour and fluoresces, mapping the failure.
In sample X-rays a gorgeous orange flares
in the rat's cancerous right leg.
Like pollen on a bee's hindquarters, exactly there.

When the bees came home to the red comb,
the last light shone through their stained
stomachs. So I wonder,
what does it mean to bond with a tumour?
Perhaps there's less harm in it than I thought.

I didn't want to believe it, said the apiarist.

Neither did I,
but a strange love has often been my saviour,
so I wasn't entirely against it either.

On the *Meditations*[*]

1. *I will suppose that the sky, the air, the Earth, colours, figures, sounds, and all external things, are nothing better than the illusions of dreams....*

2. A philosopher's first premise is his act of faith.

3. Descartes's first premise: doubt. Its corollary: solitude.

4. *I have opportunely freed my mind from all cares [and am happily disturbed by no passions]....*

5. René had a "niece," Francine, whom he adored. (She could not be "daughter" for her "mother" was the servant girl.)

6. Just as the first critics opened the *Meditations*, Francine died of scarlet fever.

7. René, distraught, wrote to his father when she died; by the time the letter arrived, there was no father to read it.

8. Then his sister died too.

9. *...in amazement I almost persuade myself that I am now dreaming.*

10. The *Meditations*, though already circulating, feels like an act of mourning.

11. *I will consider myself as without hands, eyes, flesh, blood, or any of the senses....*

---

[*] "On the *Meditations*" uses excerpts from Descartes's "First Meditation," his "Synopsis of the Meditations," and a letter to Chanut, dated June 15, 1646, all translated by Jon Veitch.

12. A call to strip down, to tear away garments already half torn.

13. *... it follows that the body may, indeed, without difficulty perish, but that the mind is in its own nature immortal.*

14. Imagine a man lifting his daughter's coffin, taking the weight of it onto fleshless, bloodless shoulders.

15. Happily disturbed by no passions.

16. *For I am assured that... there will arise neither peril nor error from this course....*

17. Francine, of course, had been both error and peril.

18. Facing death, he later wrote, was much easier and more sure than believing in preservation of life.

19. Imagine a man whose body, even in grief, bears the full load of his mind.

20. Imagine an error from which he never quite recovers.

Missing

Lauren is gorgous — scraped into the paint
on a metal door near the high school. I don't know
Lauren, but I believe it. Who isn't today?
The trickling sounds of windblown
meltwater everywhere,
and every one of us missing a vowel.

Ovid would have approved:
this is how to chronicle beauty: scratch it in.
Show the something it takes from you that makes you
ache a little, O avid one, most lovely vandal.

And if your ode hints at gorgons,
so much the better — we need their boldness
to dare use words like *shimmering, luminous.*

Droplets fall in sheaves from the gutters.
The day's missing vowel expands in the sky
all afternoon, giving off a light that dissolves
in water as Latin dissolves
into all the modern Romance languages.

Look up, gorgous Lauren: the day awaits you.

Fear of Wasps

He tried to explain it to me,
how his friend fell off his bike
and broke his clavicle after a wasp
flew up his shirt and stung him
repeatedly, continuing to sting him
even after he had fallen
into the ditch and lay in the dirt
howling, while my friend laughed
at him, doubled over,
reaching out half-heartedly
but too weak to clasp
his friend's outstretched hand.

The story told me almost nothing
about wasps. But his failure
to grasp his friend's hand puts me
in mind of Adam's finger
almost but not quite touching God's.
And perhaps the wasps are somehow
the embodiment of the space
between those two hands, that inch
of not-being. They are the gap
my friend fears in the world — flying zeroes,
buzzing nihilists — their carrion-loving bodies
a lacuna carried from one day into the next.
It's not a fear of being stung but of being stung
and reaching out and finding nothing there,
for he loved his friend
but despised him in equal measure,
and the gap between these things
he cannot account for.

How to Be Hungry

The bees have left the flowers.
The flowers have turned to wallpaper.
The wallpaper yellows.

A man sits in his chair all morning.
It feels like it takes that long to imagine doing
anything. His tea is cold,
the honey still open beside him.
He has forgotten how to be hungry.

His window has ceased to be a view,
is now a space through which
something will enter.
He coughs. Coughs again.
Come in. Nothing there.
Come in. Nothing.
He stirs, angry now, feels for a cup to bang —
Come in I say! A car horn blares.
His eyes roam the room,
his arm drops to his side.
He's too tired for this.
The honey crystallizes,
eats the light grain by grain,
forcing it down
to the bottom of the jar
where its bright gaze hardens.

Notre-Dame de Paris

The flashes going off every few
seconds, pale moths fluttering

in the hundreds, battering
the pews but disappearing before

they reach the ceiling's high arch.
A kind of migration, echoed

in the rustling of thin pages,
guidebooks in a dozen languages

talking together, wondering why
history is not enough,

why we cling to the dream of heaven,
for each flash releases

such a dream. Our faces are weak
and uncertain: death wanders through

them like a tourist, even here,
where we tilt our heads back and listen

to the rustling pages
and all the other noises we try

not to make — squeaking
sneakers, crinkling Gore-Tex —

rise, drift up to the domed ceiling
and hang there, accidental prayers

of no consequence
but carried up none the less.

Guardians

All winter, the slow drag
of a door opening.
Now silence.

Trees stagger under their
newfound weight,
stunned, the light already
laying waste.

I'd like to step in,
take their place.
Instead I raise my eyes
to the steady, gas-blue
flame of the sky:
spare me, don't spare me.

Exercise in Beauty No. 2*

I took a lighter to a seagull feather, seeking a glimpse
of what E. had witnessed. I was reading Farrokhzad
at the time:

*commit flight to memory,
for the bird is mortal.*

It seemed to me that flight was equally
mortal, and memory, for all its fallibility,
indeed the best bet:

when E. was a girl in Poland, she said, the barn
down the hill caught
fire. She watched in her nightdress, beaming like Caesar
as chickens plunged from the hayloft into the freakish glow
of the fire trucks,

plumage consumed mid-flight, wings flapping uselessly,
which is one definition of beauty —
uselessness — or so you might think. *What kind of person
are you?* her mother demanded. Even now

E. struggles to tell the difference between affliction
and miracle. She still dreams about the chickens: flailing,

they scribbled themselves across the sky,
birds and flight partially immortalized
by the fire's mnemonics.

---

* The second stanza is from "I'm Depressed" by Forugh Farrokhzad, translated from the
Persian by Michael C. Hillmann.

The gull feather in my hand burned so fast that
birth and death seemed compressed
in a single instant;
I remember
it was gone almost before I lifted my thumb
from the flint wheel.

Cherry Trees

A blur of white, pre-photogenic.
Ships bound for distant shores.

A hint of nostalgia
that isn't an escape — or if it is,
I escape only into the here and now,
only into this same place
cast in another light.

The trees stand unblinking,
pull down so much sun they seem
finally to disappear in it, become
a deficiency, pale, forgetful.
They gather absence around them
and are strangely increased by it
in a way I envy.

It feels like someone has laid their head
on my shoulder. And it weighs
nothing at all.

Summer, Madrid

The woman unfolds her fan.

It has waited, cradled
in her purse all morning.

Every slender rib
another Eve.

She can tell it's been talking
with the dead again:

the lacquered poppies
have been blowing in the fields.

Mezquita–Cathedral*
Córdoba, Spain

Reckless hybrid,
monster-child of warfarers,
Romans, Visigoths, Muslims, Catholics:

nineteen of the Moorish doors sealed,
the old light banished. But endless arcades
line the hypostyle halls, striped voussoirs echoing
the infinite — wave upon wave gallops,
resolute,
        over repurposed columns of granite, marble,
jasper, onyx —

The horizon, though, twists
suddenly, turns the eye
toward the Christian God above,
from Allah to the angels,
the floor forced
to gather itself and rise
into a Renaissance peak,

a golden, giddying
shell-like spurl that swells
skyward, almost vanishing into
its predicted paradise.

Yet even King Charles
felt his triumph poor:

---

* The image and italicized line in stanza seven are from Urdu poet Muhammad Iqbal's poem "The Mosque of Cordoba," written in the early 1930s and translated by Saleem A. Gilani. Muslims are currently petitioning for the right to pray in the Mezquita.

if divine truth can be
split like this, pitted against itself
in such a crusade,

if a drop of the lifeblood
can indeed transform *a piece of dead rock
into a living heart*

and if so beautiful a heart can lie
in the still-beautiful body of its
slain adversary, what then?

The very fabric of the universe
plunged into internecine battle, a clash
so fundamental it plays out as geometry:
the x-axis at war with the y,

a horizontal eternity invaded
by the vertical.

Magnificent eyesore,
ungodly god:

the enemy keeps on coming.

Between Heaven and Earth

The angels console one another, their wings crusted
with salt, their robes dusty from trailing
in the earth. They droop as though malnourished,
feeling the absence of the light we borrow from them
every time we cry out for more than has been given.
Tired, they are very tired
but they —
and they —
neither *but* nor *and* suffices for what marries them
to their tiredness, their faces soft,
faintly outlined
as though faded by eternities of wind and rain.
They hear the ticking of hearts;
it fills the empty quarries of their chests,
unfinished rhythms calling them down.
Their task: to sing the failed centuries,
the dark, burnt light buried
under the leafy humus of distant decades,
recalling all those left to rot, sinking into their fate
while the bodies of their children grow heavier.
Without the angels' voices, their emptiness
leaving a gap in the day,
we couldn't manage more than a glance backward,
our faces pushed hard into the autumnal light.
If they have a grievance they keep it hidden,
bury it in the unmarked cemeteries
that lie, untended, in the backs of our minds.
They visit on our behalf, stand on
the graves like missing headstones.
We owe them everything.

Prelude

Late-afternoon antique light:
the peonies lean forward as though they were letting someone fasten or unfasten a
necklace
and fell asleep halfway through,
 narcoleptic,
for, like anything beautiful,
they seem under the influence, succumb to the pace of their fleet selves
so that every moment slows and quiets and builds against itself,
enlarging like the sound
of a dripping faucet in an empty apartment,
the moment an expanded version of itself
with room to close your eyes and breathe the deep, easy breath of sleep.

All the while, though,
almost forgotten, what doesn't cease
is the blooming, the endless somnambulant begetting, petals accumulating like
the hymns that, obsessed by a single word, can't stop repeating it.
Each heavy head is a storm gathering silently on the horizon, somewhere faraway,

and even then it seems to have slowed, somehow, taking its time,
as though the storm will never come, not now, not to us, not in this life —

Nature is not the infinite but its prelude;
        that's what Schiller thought,
                and the peonies, no surprise, have begun to wilt;
I can see ants on the stems, can see them beginning to lose not just their conscious but also their unconscious souls.
But what if they don't, what if instead they just kept on growing,

as though no one were waiting for them to take their last slow breaths,
    not us, not anyone,
and they will have a chance to complete themselves, opening until they span the horizons, dizzyingly,
until there is nothing that does not open with them — and if they sometimes bend a little, droop, if an ant still clings to a stem,
it's nothing to worry about.

It's just the memory of what things used to be like.

Poem for Nietzsche's Eyes*

My office was once a girl's room — a little swallow
cut from a mirror is still glued to the wall. At night

in the window's doubled panes, I can see the swallow
and a twin, flying in perfect formation, steadily

into the darkness. I'm watching Nietzsche this evening,
replaying one minute and sixteen seconds of snowy footage,

his huge, steady nineteenth-century eyes looming
from a sickbed in Weimar, indifferent to the aphrodisiacal

light that fell into the room. *Forgive me, my friends,*
I have ventured to paint my happiness on the wall.

He lay as though finally convinced the wall was out of reach.
And the swallows, he could no longer picture them.

Last night, snow slid from the roof with a crash
that shook the house. The footage flickers irresolutely

on the screen; I watch from deep inside the winter
of 2012. The snow drifts. The swallows don't move unless I do.

---

* "Poem for Nietzsche's Eyes" is for Frances Wright, with thanks for the loan of her room. The italicized sentence is the last sentence in book 1 of Nietzsche's *The Gay Science*.

What Can I Tell You

I was hopeless
on the playground,
too quick to hold the hand
of anyone who looked sad.
It was the wrong thing to do,
didn't help any of us.
Yet I miss my childhood.

What can I tell you:
as I grow older
I begin to understand why
there is a Christ on a cross.
I don't know what to do.
I don't know how
to suffer that much
and am afraid.

My Name*

"Martha, Martha," the Lord answered, "you are worried and upset about many things."
 — Luke 10:41-42

He said it twice:
Martha, Martha.

That made it easy.
I understood.

Listen, hear how his voice
drops, deepens the second time:
Martha.

As though he were laying something down,
something he'd taken from me
which was too heavy for me,
too heavy for him as well.

If a name spoken once is a claim,
twice is the claim undone.

Twice is love.

They said he could walk on water.
I believe that now.

I wanted to speak his name
but hadn't the strength.
That's why, since he left,
I cannot go about my work.

---

* The epigraph comes from the New International translation of the Bible.

I stand in the kitchen,
reciting pairs of names,

fish, fish,
fork, fork,
stone, stone,
spider, spider,

trying to match
the timbre of my voice to his
so the thing named
settles,

so my troubles subside
and he too comes to rest:

Lord, Lord.

Visited*

There's a painting of Joan of Arc in which golden
people float in the trees behind her. She looks
as though she sees them.

She is God's summer home, her eyes a bay on which he floats
for a time of an afternoon.

Holy-crazy is the look in her eyes.

One summer, the whales came to the cliffs behind
my mother's home. I was in the garden and heard them singing;
it was like hearing voices, the sound seemed to come
from nowhere and everywhere.

Their flukes ghostly as they floated up to the surface.

My eyes fell over the cliff and into the bellies
of those whales, who have never returned.

---

* The painting referred to is *Joan of Arc* (1879) by Jules Bastien-Lepage.

The Dead

This morning, the obdurate, golden-green grass, blurred with dew,
buried in the house's shadow.
Deer, their faces softened by sleep, raise their heads and look through you,
draining you of motive.
You become as still as they are, waiting,
as though under it all lurked another, more comprehensible world,
                            carrying itself so slowly

as to go unnoticed.

*

What if the dead don't leave,
                    not exactly;
what if instead they're what orients you, the sixth sense that turns you
this way and that,
tilts your face toward the light? What if they *are* the light?
That would explain, wouldn't it,
the strange clarity after someone dies,

the peculiar radiance things acquire, even the least of them,
your loss everywhere transformed,
your suffering grown impersonal, self-sufficient.
Each item buzzes with the vibrancy
of the one who's gone —   an inherited light that is no longer
theirs, that only you still recognize —
so every time you close your eyes something of that person
leaves again.

*

Let's be clear:
about the stillness you felt in the deer this morning —
and yes, you're still staring, still feel the lukewarm glass against your forehead
as you think of the dew and of the grass and of the deer themselves,
now vanished from the lawn: it had nothing to do with the dead.

The dead don't stop
with their hearts in their throats; to die

is not to wash through the body of a deer like a ghost;
it isn't to skulk under a living skin.
It's a change in the value of things.
There's no such thing as "the dead":
when the dead die, they don't hold anything back.
Otherwise, a bitterness, like the sediment
in wine.

    It's pure alchemy:
the world pours itself into the vessel of the new day,
and the liquid runs clear.

And that's what hurts.
The clarity. It leaves you staring out the window,
wondering what to forgive: the lawn more beautiful than it should be,
the blades of grass all
bent one way, silvered and utterly coherent,
like a mirror with no face in it.

Acknowledgements

It's hard to wrap my head around the many, many places, beings, and ecologies that have enabled me to write the poems that make up this book. Among them I acknowledge, in particular, the Beothuk territory on which I was mostly raised and the unceded Wəlastəkwiyik territory of the "beautiful river" where I live now and where the new poems in this book were written. These have been life-giving places in which to dwell.

I thank everyone in my family for their love and support. Nick, how lucky am I to love and live with someone who inhabits so many of the same joys and concerns as I do, and who is also patient with the differences between us. Abigail, thank you for moments like seeing, in a red leaf with a curved stem, a fox and its tail. I love moving through the world with you.

I was lucky enough to spend years learning the art of poetic attention from Don McKay and Jan Zwicky, and I'm conscious every day of what they've given me to live up to.

I thank my other past editor, River Guri, for their good guidance, and particularly Ross Leckie, who, among other things, proposed this book to me then did the work to make it a real thing, and who has been an unstintingly generous presence as long as I've known him.

More thanks go to Alayna Munce, who has read and edited so many of these poems and whom I love. Also to Brick Books and Goose Lane Editions for publishing the original books from which this collection draws. Still more thanks to Alan, Julie, Martin, and James at Goose Lane for their work on the production of this book.

My gratitude to *ARC Magazine*, *Grain*, the *Malahat Review*, *Prairie Fire*, *Qwerty*, *TNQ*, *Women & Environments*, and the *Walrus*, where some of the new poems in this collection were first published. Thanks also to the editors of *Cadence* for including three of these new poems in their anthology. And thanks to the Andrew and Laura McCain Art Gallery in Florenceville-Bristol, New Brunswick, for commissioning "Thoughts and Prayers."

Finally, I thank the students I've been lucky enough to work with over the last several years. It's been a privilege and a joy.

Sue Sinclair is the author of five books of poetry. Her debut collection, *Secrets of Weather & Hope* (2001), was shortlisted for the Gerald Lampert Award, while her second book, *Mortal Arguments* (2003), was a *Globe & Mail* Top 100 Book and appeared on the shortlist for the Atlantic Poetry Prize. *The Drunken Lovely Bird* (2005) won the IPPY Poetry Award from the American Independent Publishers' Association and was shortlisted for both the Pat Lowther Award and the Acorn-Plantos People's Poetry Prize. It was followed in 2008 by *Breaker*, which was shortlisted for the Pat Lowther Award and the Atlantic Poetry Prize, and in 2016 by her most recent collection, *Heaven's Thieves*, which won the Pat Lowther Award.

Sinclair's poetry has been published in magazines and journals across Canada and the US. Her poem "Home from Danceland" inspired the dance production *A Turn on the Floor* by PushPULL Dance Co., and poems from *Breaker* provided inspiration for a series of musical compositions by modern Canadian composer Emilie Cecilia LeBel. Sinclair holds a PhD in philosophy from the University of Toronto and currently teaches creative writing at the University of New Brunswick. She was inaugural critic-in-residence for CWILA (Canadian Women in the Literary Arts). She is also a poetry editor for Brick Books and the editor of the *Fiddlehead*.

Photo: Peter Sinclair